Irresistible
Revitalize and Empower Your Marriage

JIM HOHNBERGER

Pacific Press® Publishing Association
Nampa, Idaho
Oshawa, Ontario, Canada
www.pacificpress.com

Also by Jim Hohnberger

Escape to God

Empowered Living

It's About People

Come to the Quiet

Men of Power

Facing Frenemy Fire

Dedication

If you have fallen out of love, have hit a plateau, or find yourselves just going through the motions . . .

If you love each other—but want to be "in love" again . . .

If you are looking for a life partner and deeply desire a marriage that stays irresistible . . .

I dedicate this book to you.

Acknowledgments

Where would one be without his right hand? How much does one value and depend upon it?

When it comes to the writing of my books, Jeanette Houghtelling is my right hand. She's always there, creatively turning my black and white into living color.

Praise God for right hands!

Special thanks and appreciation to Milton and Arleta Afonso for so graciously providing their little "Eden" getaway as a base where I could write this book.

Cover design by Steve Lanto
Cover resources from dreamstime.com
Inside design by Aaron Troia

Copyright © 2009 by
Jim Hohnberger
Printed in the United States of America
All rights reserved

Unless otherwise noted, Scriptures are quoted from The New King James Version, copyright © 1979, 1980, 1982, Thomas Nelson, Inc., Publishers.

Scripture quoted from NASB are from *The New American Standard Bible*®, Copyright © 1960, 1962, 1963, 1968, 1971, 1972, 1973, 1975, 1977, 1995 by The Lockman Foundation. Used by permission.

Scripture quotations marked NIV are from the HOLY BIBLE, NEW INTERNATIONAL VERSION®. Copyright © 1973, 1978, 1984 by International Bible Society. Used by permission of Zondervan Publishing House. All rights reserved.

Scripture quotations marked NLT are taken from the Holy Bible, New Living Translation, copyright © 1996, 2004. Used by permission of Tyndale House Publishers, Inc., Wheaton, Illinois 60189. All rights reserved.

Additional copies of this book are available by calling toll-free 1-800-765-6955 or by visiting www.adventistbookcenter.com.

Library of Congress Cataloging-in-Publication Data

Hohnberger, Jim, 1948-
  Irresistible : revitalize and empower your marriage / Jim Hohnberger.
      p. cm.
  ISBN 13: 978-0-8163-2331-9 (hard cover)
  ISBN 10: 0-8163-2331-3
  1. Marriage—Religious aspects—Christianity. I. Title.
  BV835.H633 2009
  248.8'44—dc22

                                                         2008049591

09 10 11 12 13 • 5 4 3 2 1

Contents

1. Irresistibly in Love 7

2. The Fountain of Irresistibility....................................20

3. Becoming Irresistible...37

4. Focused on Her 52

5. Focused on Him 66

6. Love Is Extravagant..80

7. Love Killers...97

8. Stalled..110

9. From Incompatible to Irresistible..........................125

10. Pass It On!..140

Bonus Chapter: Guidelines for Young Lovers 146

*From J. D. and Alecia's wedding invitation, February 2008—
irresistibly in love!*

CHAPTER 1

Irresistibly in Love

And now abide faith, hope, love, these three; but the greatest of these is love.

—1 Corinthians 13:13

I held their wedding announcement in my hands. It had arrived tucked in the middle of the usual stack of catalogs, advertisements, bills, and ministry mail that is delivered twice a week to our wilderness home. I usually sort through all that stuff very quickly, tossing most of it, and scanning the rest, prioritizing my responses. But as I opened their announcement, I forgot about efficiency.

It wasn't that their announcement was cleverly designed. Actually, it was rather simple. Black print on ordinary white cardstock, it appeared to have been produced on a home computer. But there was an elegance about this invitation that eclipsed the lack of fancy paper and stylish design.

It was the picture of J. D. and Alecia that caught my eye. J. D. was tall, handsome, and well built. Alecia was slender, with dark, wavy hair flowing to her waist. Profiled against a snow-covered fence and fir trees, apparently oblivious to winter cold and falling snowflakes, J. D. had scooped Alecia into his arms. She nestled against his chest with arms entwined around his neck. No doubt about it, J. D., twenty-one, and Alecia, nineteen, made an attractive couple. Sally and I had known Alecia's family for years and had watched her blossom from a cute little girl into a lovely young woman.

My eyes lingered on the invitation. Something more than their attractiveness drew me to them—something intangible and yet very real. They were in love! Irresistibly in love! Their faces radiated with it. The smiles . . . the eyes . . . there was a glow that spoke more than words. It wasn't something they put on for the camera. There was nothing stiff or formal about them. Their love was real, sweet, fresh, and it was happening now. Their hearts were connected in a way they had never experienced before and neither of them wanted this moment to fade.

A few days later, my phone rang. "Mr. Hohnberger, this is Alecia. J. D. and I would like some marriage counseling. Our parents think it would be good for us. Would you be available to help us?"

"Now Alecia, I'd be happy to spend some time with you and J. D., but I want to ask you something first."

"What's that?" she returned a bit suspiciously.

"Are you calling only to appease your parents or do you and J. D. really want some counseling?"

She giggled. "Well, kind of . . . both."

"That's all right. What kind of counseling would you like? We can explore your compatibility with J. D. or talk about courtship or—"

"No, Mr. Hohnberger," she broke in. "We don't want to discuss those things. Our wedding date is less than three months away. We just want to know how to keep a marriage together." I could sense her unspoken plea: *Please don't burst our bubble.*

We agreed on a time for the two of them to visit our home and chat. "You and J. D. write down the questions you have about marriage, and we'll talk about those when you come," I suggested.

The interview

I could feel the electricity when they walked hand in hand through our back door. There were those sparkling eyes and glowing smiles I had been so drawn to in their wedding announcement. Their "tingles" were almost contagious—so fresh, pure, and self-evident. You know what I mean by "tingles," don't you? The chemistry was working, making them feel more alive than they'd ever felt before. To them, all things seemed possible! Mount Everest would be a small obstacle for their love. It was exhilarating, intoxicating!

J. D. and Alecia's feet hardly touched the ground—they were so enamored with each other. They seemed to have not a care in the world. I offered them their choice of seats in the living room and, of course, they chose the sofa where she could cozy up under his arm. I wondered if they would have the presence of mind to engage in meaningful conversation. So often the "tingles" become blinders to the realities of life and relationships. Would their questions take us to any real depth? I was to be pleasantly surprised.

Question one

After we chatted for a few moments about the drive up our snowy, wilderness road, I got down to business. "So what questions do you two lovebirds have for me today?"

Irresistibly in Love

J. D. cleared his throat and glanced down at the pad of paper they had brought with them. Looking back at me, he blushed slightly and began. "Mr. Hohnberger, will the 'tingles' go away? I mean, Alecia and I are so in love—does that have to stop? Everyone says it will. And that does seem to be true for most people. Most marriages we've seen, except for yours, seem to have lost that 'in love' experience. In fact, we know few marriages in the church or out of the church that are happy, vibrant, or what we want for ourselves."

I was astonished at the question and their perception of the state of most marriages. Indeed, they were right on!

Willard Harley, in the preface to *His Needs, Her Needs,* points out that the divorce rate among all groups in America climbed from 10 percent in 1960 to around 50 percent in 1980 and that the percentage of single adults increased from 6.5 percent to 20 percent. The divorce rate somewhat stabilized in 1980, but the percentage of single adults has continued to climb to about 30 percent because fewer people are willing to commit themselves to one partner for life.[1]

But J. D. and Alecia both came from conservative Christian homes with high standards. Surely they would be immune to those trends. Not so. According to the Barna Research Group, "Born-again Christians are just as likely to divorce as are non-Christians."[2] "Born again Christians . . . were indistinguishable from the national average on the matter of divorce."[3]

In addition to these disturbing trends, only a minority of couples who stay together are satisfied with their marriages. Years ago, Ann Landers reported the results of an informal poll she took among her readers. Her question, "If you had it to do all over again, would you marry the same person?" drew an avalanche of replies. Shockingly, 70 percent said No, they would not marry the person they had married.[4] A recent survey by AOL, in conjunction with *Woman's Day* magazine asked its readers the same question, "If you had it to do all over again, would you marry the same husband?" Thirty-six percent said No; 20 percent said they weren't sure; and only 44 percent said Yes.[5] This correlates with what Sally and I have observed as we

---

1. Willard Harley, *His Needs, Her Needs: How to Affair-Proof Your Marriage* (Grand Rapids, Mich.: Fleming H. Revell, 2001), 9.
2. The Barna Update, September 8, 2004. www.barna.org.
3. The Barna Update, March 31, 2008. www.barna.org.
4. Sylvia Weishaus and Dorothy Field, "A Half Century of Marriage: Continuity or Change?" *Journal of Marriage and the Family,* vol. 50, no. 3 (August 1988): 763–74. Quoted in *Before You Get Engaged,* by Gudgel and Gudgel.
5. http://www.womansday.com/home/11092/behind-closed-doors-a-womans-day-and-aol-survey.html.

have talked with hundreds of couples across North and South America, Europe, and the South Pacific. Few marriages that we have seen could be characterized as genuinely happy.

What J. D. and Alecia observed agrees with the statistics; and yet it ought not to be this way—not in the church of Christ! Christian marriages should be the example for the world. "And now abide faith, hope, love."[6] Our faith and hope should produce a dynamic love that is different and distinct from that of the world—and our marriages should be the showcases of that love. If they're not, perhaps our faith and hope in a living Savior is but mere form, weekly ritual, and bare mental assent.

I looked into J. D. and Alecia's eyes—eyes full of faith, hope, and love, mingled with questions. Faith that God meant marriage to be a lasting love story. Hope that they could experience God's intention for them—a vibrant love that sends tingles all the way down to their toes. And questions, Could it work for them?

"Yes, J. D. and Alecia," I replied to their original question, "the 'tingles' you are experiencing will likely mellow in time, but that doesn't have to be the end of love. It can be just the beginning of a deeper, intentional love—a love that, if nurtured, will grow brighter and deeper than what you are now experiencing."

Dr. Pat Love has written about four stages of love.[7] It's helpful to understand them because it puts in perspective the highs and lows of committed love.

1. Infatuation. This is the stage I call the "tingles," when the chemistry between a man and a woman comes alive. And it truly is based on chemistry. The attraction between two people actually causes their bodies to produce a "love potion" made up of chemicals that have a powerful influence on their brains. Michael Liebowitz, a research psychiatrist at the New York State Psychiatric Institute, explains that when we come into contact with a person who highly attracts us, our brain becomes saturated with a love cocktail comprised of PEA and several other excitatory neurotransmitters, including dopamine and norepinephrine. PEA, known as the "love molecule," works in concert with dopamine and norepinephrine and triggers incredible side effects. Symptoms include a delightfully positive attitude, increased energy, decreased need for sleep, and loss of appetite. Increased concentrations of dopamine in the brain are associated with euphoria. Norepinephrine, which is chemically derived from dopamine, is generally associated with exhilaration, excessive energy, and other excitatory responses.

---

6. 1 Corinthians 13:13.

7. Pat Love, *The Truth About Love: The Highs, the Lows, and How You Can Make It Last Forever* (N.Y.: Simon & Schuster, 2001).

Sound familiar? We've all known someone caught in the throes of infatuation. The strong, silent man becomes expressive and thoughtful. The woman who spends her free time sewing suddenly begins exploring the great outdoors. The "regular schedule" fanatic starts relishing leisurely moonlight walks far past bedtime. They find it easy to overlook even glaring faults in their beloved—optimistically believing they can work out any difficulties that may arise.

Eventually, however, the flood of chemicals wanes and with it, the "tingles." The couple enters the second stage of their relationship.

2. Post-rapture. What an unromantic word! This stage can be a bit disconcerting—especially if it happens after the couple gets married. When the effects of the "love potion" are no longer felt, both partners go back to their former behaviors. The strong, silent man talks less; the sedentary woman loses her fascination for the woods; and the scheduled person gets back on track. Each begins to realize the need to catch up on responsibilities he or she neglected while so enamored with each other.

For most, the transition to this stage takes place over time. Little habits they once found endearing start to be annoying. Differences in tastes, needs, and ideas become more pronounced. Once they were willing to give limitlessly, now they don't always want to give because they feel they aren't getting as much in return. Once conversation had been effortless, now they experience more silence between them. They feel a greater need for space and private time. Worst of all, they tend not to give each other the benefit of the doubt.

At this point, some couples conclude they've made a terrible mistake. They spread their wings and take flight. Others accept the changes and settle in to endure "reality." For Sally and me, I would call this stage the "Convenience Stage." I began to treat Sally like a convenience—something to make my life more comfortable—and she quietly complied. Fortunately, God woke us up and helped us to move into the next two stages—which I call "Intentional Love."

3. Discovery. Sally and I did a lot of "discovering" during the first few months of our "swing time"! What is "swing time"? When we left the suburbs of Appleton, Wisconsin, and moved to the mountains of Montana, I decided to make rediscovering my wife's heart my business. So every day at noon, we would sit in the swing my son built in our front yard and talk—I mean, *really* talk. As Sally began to open up, I did a lot of discovering. And she did too.

It's important for couples to discover—in a very real way—each other's strengths, weaknesses, and needs. Without the tingles-induced, rose-colored glasses, we see each other more realistically. Each has made assumptions about the other, and both have expectations that need to be communicated and worked out. These include clarifying roles for such things as who takes out the trash or writes the checks. Husbands and wives must learn how to communicate love to one another effectively and continue to build trust based on mutual commitment. This leads to the best and most enduring stage of love, which is

4. *Connection.* Connection combines the best of the "tingles" with the journey of discovery. At this stage, the couple builds a true friendship with each other, works as a team to make their home a safe haven, and provides support for each other. They construct a connection that stands the test of time and proves even more satisfying than the "high" of infatuation.

I met just such a couple recently. Sagging, wrinkled, and shapeless would be honest adjectives for Evelyn's eighty-year-old face and figure. Yet when George looked at her, he was obviously enraptured. In his eyes, no twenty-year-old could hold a candle to his Evelyn. I used to wonder how that could be! Now I know. The profound connection those two had forged through the crucible of life—the highs and the lows—was, for them, an incomparable treasure that transcended all other attractions!

Near the ending point?

As we talked about these four stages of marriage, Alecia looked troubled. "Well then, Mr. Hohnberger, does every marriage have to come near the ending point before things get worked out?"

"Absolutely *not*!" I assured her. "If both of you will apply two simple principles every day and are willing to pay the price, your wedding day can be but the beginning of irresistible love—not the end. You will undoubtedly go through some low spots in your relationship, but if both of you will always come back to applying these two principles, you will weather the storms and develop a deep, connected love that is even more satisfying than what you feel right now!"

I wish you could have seen how their questioning expressions became radiant as they realized that their union of heart and life could be an exception to the norm for marriages both in the church and in the world. Now their faith had a new hope that their love could be a different kind of love—a love that would press through difficulties and actually grow deeper than the love they were experiencing now. Of course, they wanted to know what these two principles were that I referred to. I shared them with J. D. and Alecia, and I'll tell you about them shortly too. But first I want to introduce you to two other couples.

Incompatible

Why they ever got married, I'll never know! I've never seen a couple more incompatible than Stan and Susan. They fought daily—continuously—like two bulldogs! They engaged in a constant tug-of-war over values and lifestyle.

Susan was religious; Stan had no use for the pharisaical, hypercritical, reform-minded, church-going crowd Susan hung out with. She was a health enthusiast; he loved his junk food. She was a dress reformer; he thought a suit was something the undertaker dresses you in for your coffin. She was an earnest, conservative, church-going, Bible believer; he was into pornography, Hollywood movies, and competitive sports. She conscientiously home-schooled their two children; he would rather just send them off to public school and let the teachers deal with them.

Stan spent his free time in front of the TV and on the Internet. "Family time?" Stan scoffed. "Forget it! I'm going to do what I'm going to do. You raise the kids, and I'll bring home the bacon." He was brash, determined, and dug in. Susan really tried. She'd drag Stan to our meetings, and he'd walk out and drive home, leaving her to find her own way home.

Then one day, I received a phone call.

"Jim, I need your help," Stan begged anxiously. "Susan has left me and taken the two children with her. She emptied our bank account and moved out of state. She won't talk to me; she's filing for divorce. Her family hates me and wants her to dump me. Most of her church supports her—except for a few who think she is a fanatic. Her attorney says I have two options: divorce or talk to you. Can you help me?"

I paused as I sent up a silent petition to God. "Well, Stan, yes and no. Yes, I can offer some help if both you and Susan will agree to do just two things for ninety days. But if you won't, there isn't much hope at all. Your marriage will go the route of other broken homes."

"Anything, Jim. I'll do anything." Stan's voice broke, and he began to sob. "I just can't bear the thought of losing my family!"

I couldn't believe what I was hearing. It had been obvious to me for quite some time that Susan and Stan had been barreling headlong down a collision course with divorce. Hadn't it been obvious to him? I had to ask.

"Stan, why did you wait so long before you were ready to repair this marriage?"

He choked up again. "I just never thought Susan would leave me and take the children and our savings. I guess it really woke me up." He swallowed hard. "Tell me, Jim, what are these two things that will save my marriage?"

"I want to share these two principles with the two of you together. Can you and Susan set up a conference call with me sometime this week?"

They both called—he from their empty house, and she from her parents' home—and what a call that was! Stan had gone from the extreme of belligerence to near groveling, while Susan's desperate determination had grown to defiance. He wanted her back, but she was done! He pled with tears for her to try "just one more time." He would do anything, make any change, if only she would come home.

"Forget it!" Susan snapped. "I won't try again until I see evidence that you're changing! Get rid of the TV, the Internet, and your junk food. Start going to church and reading your Bible, and I'll think about it."

But this was too much for Stan. His approach quickly changed from groveling to growling, and the two bulldogs were again at each other's throats. I abruptly interrupted them. "Listen, you two, if you want to head for divorce court, I'll just get off the phone, and you can do that. But if you want to give your marriage a chance, you both must be willing to listen and try another approach. Now, which will it be?"

Silence.

Stan spoke first. "Sorry, Jim. I'm ready to listen."

"Susan?" I queried. "What about you?"

She sighed. "OK, go ahead."

I shared with Susan and Stan a basic two-step, ninety-day solution. And after working through many tears and a lot of reluctance, they both agreed to try—for ninety days. Stan was at the end of his rope and ready to try anything. Susan reasoned that she didn't have a lot to lose if she put off the divorce for another ninety days—and there was a teensy-weensy, tiny possibility that it might work. She might as well give it a try.

They both entered into the process and honestly tried. Oh, they had a lot of stumbles. Like a child learning to walk, they had to get up again and again and again. Old ways conflicted with new principles. Frustrations and distractions mingled with victories. The highs and lows of their emotions took them on quite a roller-coaster ride. But they didn't give up.

They would call every week to report their progress. I encouraged them, pointing out that God doesn't necessarily care how many times we fall, but how many times we get back up. God understands the process and sees us as we will be at the end of the experience. I encouraged them to stay with the two divine principles. "Don't get discouraged. You can learn a new way of thinking and responding."

And they did!

After the ninety days, I asked them to give their testimony at one of our camp meetings they were planning to attend. As they came forward to join me on the platform, I couldn't help seeing the transformation. Instead of bristling at each other like bulldogs, they seemed calm, peaceful—even happy!

Stan and Susan shared amidst tears their "before" and "after." When they were finished, I asked, "Stan, on a scale of one to ten, with ten being the highest, what is your marriage like now?"

"Jim, it's a twelve! I can hardly believe it!" Stan beamed from ear to ear.

I turned to Susan. Stan had his arm around her, and she glowed like a bride on her wedding day. "Susan, how would you rate your marriage?"

"Jim, it's better than our honeymoon. I never believed it could work out so well in such a short time. I'm so happy!"

In those ninety days, Stan and Susan discovered what every couple can discover. God's solutions work! They are both simple to understand and far-reaching in their application. They not only solve marital problems—they also restore irresistible love! The kind of love that makes your eyes sparkle and your heart flip-flop! They worked for Stan and Susan, and they will work for you as well. But first let me tell you about Bill and Barbara.

Divorced and remarried

Bill and his first wife got along all right at first. They had their ups and downs, but always managed to work through whatever came up—until Bill attended an evangelistic campaign. He had never been religious before, but a coworker he respected talked him into attending the opening night of a prophecy seminar. The information presented caught Bill's attention like nothing else he had ever known. He fell in love with the Bible and the comprehensive truths it presents. He grasped the incredible accuracy of the prophecies of Daniel and Revelation and recognized where we are in the stream of time. He was enthralled, captivated, and inspired!

He tried to get his wife to accompany him, but she wasn't interested. Disappointed, Bill attended the meetings alone—five nights a week for four weeks, and every night he came home enthusiastic. He was excited about what he was learning, and he wanted his wife to share his excitement. She resisted. He pushed. They'd get in an argument and go to bed with it unresolved. Bill began "Bible-thumping" his wife, and the walls went up. She grew cold and resentful.

You see, Bill had been converted to biblical facts, but his heart had not yet been converted to Jesus. His new knowledge made him feel morally superior to his wife, and that didn't win her heart—to him or to God. In time, Bill stopped drinking, dancing, and partying. She didn't. Bill was baptized and joined the church that had presented the seminar. His wife continued their old lifestyle until the day of their divorce.

Bill began to dream of meeting a woman that loved the truth as much as he did. Eventually, he moved to another state and found what he believed was God's answer to his longing desire—Barbara.

Barbara had been raised in "the truth" and belonged to what she termed "the remnant church." She had married within her denomination, but the marriage grew cold and ugly behind closed doors. Although her husband was a respected elder in the church and taught Bible classes, at home he was self-centered, demanding, and physically abusive to her and the children when he didn't get his way. Barbara and he had three children together, but she essentially raised them alone. Their marriage ended with his second affair. Barbara was hurting, lonely, and burdened. She began to dream of a man who could be a real companion to her.

That's when Bill arrived on the scene. Bill had no children of his own and soon became a companion and second father to Barbara's three children. It didn't take long for Barbara to feel that an empty void was being filled. She had always wanted a husband who would play with her children, take them on trips, and be a religious role model for them. Bill saw in Barbara a woman who believed as he did, attended church, and involved herself in witnessing. Within six months, they were married. They both believed God had answered their prayers and needs—and perhaps even a few of their wants, as well.

Bill and Barbara went on their honeymoon, and life was great! They had a marriage "made in heaven"—until they returned home when everything began to fall apart. It was all over the children. Barbara was permissive and indulged the children a bit too much. Bill had noticed this before he and Barbara were married and assumed that he would be her "knight in shining armor" to rescue her from the woes of an undisciplined household. Of course, he thought he was quite balanced when it came to parenting, but in reality, he was a strong, self-willed disciplinarian.

The children rebelled against Bill's rules, expectations, and consequences for noncompliance, and Barbara sympathized with her children. The children played their mother against her new husband. Bill complained that he got no respect. He felt that the children ruled the roost, and he could not tolerate such family nongovernment.

In a few short weeks, their irresistible love turned into incompatible feuds with no hope in sight. They both dug in to defend their perspectives and would consider no other alternative. This went on for years until the children left home and Barbara became involved with another man.

About this time, Sally and I were invited to the church where Bill and Barbara were members to conduct a series of meetings about walking with God and revitalizing one's marriage. As I spoke, I noticed Bill in the audience. He was listening intently. At times, I saw what might be tears in his eyes, and he leaned forward, his head in his hands, staring at the floor. It was obvious that what I was sharing stirred him deeply. He was beginning to see what he had missed—and what it had cost him.

Bill approached me between meetings and shared his heartache. "Jim, what can I do? Barbara has absolutely no interest in reconciliation. In fact, she has stopped attending church and is seeing another man. It seems like there is *no hope*!"

My heart went out to Bill. "It does appear that the odds are against you," I admitted. "But if you will implement two basic gospel principles, it's possible that you can win back your wife's heart. I can't guarantee anything—we are all free moral agents, and even God wasn't able to move Lucifer's heart."

I shared the two principles. Bill listened thoughtfully and then made a decision. "Jim, I have nothing to lose and a whole lot to gain. I've missed these simple principles all of my Christian life, thinking that my 'rightness' made *me* right. It has cost me dearly. I failed in my first marriage. I don't want to fail in this one too! I'll do it!"

Bill kept in contact with me every week. He diligently applied those two principles. Like Stan and Susan, he stumbled and had to get back up again. He rode the roller coaster of emotional ups and downs. He persevered and didn't quit. But his efforts seemed to make no difference to Barbara. She remained cold to him and enamored with the other man. Thirty days went by, sixty days, and the ninety-day mark passed.

"How are you doing, Bill?" I asked during one of our phone conversations. "You've passed the ninety-day mark, and still there are no apparent rewards for your efforts. What are you going to do?"

Without hesitation, Bill responded. "I'm going to keep going, Jim. I need to do this for my own character and for God's sake. Getting Barbara back is still incredibly important to me, but it's not my main motivation anymore. I want to walk with God and be like Him!"

Another ninety days went by. Suddenly, for some unknown reason, Barbara's relationship with the other man turned sour. She became a little more open to Bill and began to see him in a new light. Gradually, her hope was rekindled—yet she was wary. She liked the new Bill, but didn't trust the change to last. She wasn't a doubting Thomas—she was a doubting Barbara.

Bill didn't push her. He was committed to being Christlike regardless of what was in it for him. Barbara began to find Bill's new ways irresistible. Almost against her will, the barriers started coming down, and soon she found herself once again "in love."

This couple went from "incompatible" to "irresistible" because God's principles work! These two principles, once implemented, can take a marriage that is on the rocks and put it in the clouds. They will breathe fresh life into a stale marriage and bring new zest into a great marriage. They apply whether you've just celebrated your fiftieth wedding anniversary or are on your honeymoon.

They are the answer to Stan's and Susan's question, "Can our love be restored?" They give direction to Bill's plea, "Can I win my wife back?" They provide a safe guide to the next innocent question those two starry-eyed young people asked me in my living room that snowy November day, "How, then, do we *stay* in love?"

These two principles were prescribed by the One who formed Adam out of the dust of the ground, breathed life into his nostrils, and then custom-designed a companion for him from Adam's own rib. You can trust these principles because I didn't make them up! *God* is the One who prescribed them. He made us, and He knows how we operate.

The application of these two principles will create security within your marriage, and security is the basis for marriages that last. Research has shown that security is the greatest key for solid, irresistible love between you and your spouse—greater even than excellent communication skills and relationship tools. When you feel secure—and your spouse feels secure—you will stick together.[8]

Jesus summarized these two principles in these words: "You shall love the Lord your God with all your heart, with all your soul, and with all your mind. This is the first and great principle of irresistible love. And the second is like it: you shall love your spouse as yourself. On these two principles hang all the solutions to every marital difficulty."[9]

Do you think that's too simplistic? Are you skeptical? Perhaps you believe your issues are more complex. Somehow, everyone thinks he or she is a unique case. And yet God designed marriage to work within a certain framework. When we take marriage out of that framework, there are a thousand and one ways to describe how it *doesn't* work, but the core problem still remains the same—we have departed from the blueprint. The solution, then, is to get back to the original blueprint. When we do—it works!

So are you ready for the challenge?

Go ahead! Dare to be irresistible again!

---

8. That's the premise of Gary Smalley's book, *I Promise* (Nashville: Thomas Nelson, 2006).

9. Matthew 22:37–40, personal paraphrase.

Study Questions for Chapter 1

1. Would your spouse say that the two of you are presently "in love," "longing to be loved," or "out of love"?
2. Do your children desire a marriage like yours?
3. What kind of love has your faith and hope produced?
4. List the four stages of love. In which stage is your marriage?
5. Have you settled for less than best? Have you given up and thrown in the towel? Are you actively seeking solutions?
6. Will you wait until your marriage comes near the ending point before you work things out?
7. If you're near that ending point now, are you willing to apply the two principles that will really work?
8. If you are still in love, will you apply these two principles in order to build greater security into your relationship?
9. If your partner is not on board with you, will you apply these principles anyway?

CHAPTER 2

The Fountain of Irresistibility

For with You is the fountain of life.

—*Psalm 36:9*

Susan's frustration reached its peak the day before she left Stan. As usual, Stan had stumbled out of bed at the last minute, threw on the same clothes he had dropped on the floor the night before, and dashed into the kitchen to get a few bites of breakfast.

"Whole wheat pancakes with fruit topping again?" he complained. "Why can't we ever have the good stuff?"

"Why can't you at least get out of bed in time for worship?" Susan responded in kind. "You're supposed to be the priest of the house!"

"Forget it, woman. I work for a living!" And Stan dashed out the door without so much as a goodbye—much less a kiss and smile.

Susan smarted under his scathing remarks. She tried to put them aside, but her resentment toward Stan bubbled over onto her children. The children reacted by bickering with each other. When Susan began to discipline them, her oldest turned to her with fire in his eyes. "Mommy, why can't we fight? You and Daddy fight all the time!"

Stunned, Susan withdrew to her bedroom. Throwing herself on the bed, she wept bitterly. "I'm so frustrated and tired of this conflict! I just want a happy home. Why can't Stan love me and be a godly father? This just can't continue!" She slammed her fist into the pillow and then jerked herself off the bed. She stomped into the bathroom to wash her face and was startled by what she saw in the mirror. "I look more like a miserable shrew than an attractive woman," she wailed to herself. Then her anger swelled up again. "But I can't help it! If only Stan would become a godly man. If only he would play with the children when he comes home. If only he would forget about entertaining himself and read his Bible. If only he would be nice."

The Fountain of Irresistibility

She stood there seething in her resentment.

"There has to be some way to change him! I need to try to help him. Let's see. What can I do that would soften his heart so I can talk to him?"

Susan thought for a moment, and then her eyes lighted up. She had an idea. It had worked before—at least temporarily. Yes, she would try it.

Stan came home late from work, frowning and grumbling. He plopped down in his easy chair and reached for the TV remote. "What's to eat?" he wanted to know. "Not anymore of that tofu stuff, I hope!"

Without thinking, Susan snapped back, "We're having tofu lasagna. Take it or leave it!"

"I knew I should have stopped at Burger King," Stan growled.

Susan was about to tell him to go to Burger King if he liked, but she bit her tongue. Besides, Stan had already tuned her out and was caught up in a football game. She watched him for a few moments. *He's nothing but a giant amoeba,* she thought. *Oh, well, we'll see if my plan works tonight. If it doesn't, I'm out of here! No woman should have to put up with this!*

The evening passed with Stan in his own world of football and Susan in her world of children and chores. Susan had worship with the kids and tucked them in bed. By this time, Stan had moved to the office and was surfing the Internet. Susan slipped into the shower and tried to relax. After she got out, she lotioned her body, perfumed herself, and put on a slinky nightie. Tiptoeing to the office, she stepped up behind Stan. He quickly closed the window he had been looking at—but not before Susan caught a glimpse of the X-rated clip he was watching. Anger threatened to explode, but she stuffed it down. Stan turned to glance at her, gave her a once-over, and wordlessly turned back to his computer, pretending to check the weather. Susan moved closer to him and began to run her fingers through his hair.

"What d'ya want?" Stan mumbled.

"Well . . . it's been a long time since we made love. I thought—"

"No. I'm not in the mood."

Susan stiffened. He'd rather have the Internet than her! That was the last straw! Suddenly her pent-up anger exploded like Mount St. Helens. She unloaded on Stan, and he gave it right back to her with double force.

The next day, Susan left.

What's your style?

What would a day in *your* home look like? Is your marriage on a collision course with divorce like Stan's and Susan's was? Do you fight, bicker, or nag each other? Are you constantly trying to find a way to get your mate to meet your expectations and become frustrated when it doesn't work?

Perhaps overt conflict is not your style. Maybe you and your spouse carry on a "cold war." You get stuck in a stalemate, refusing to address and resolve issues.

Some marriages combine these two styles. One spouse attacks and dominates, while the other complies and withdraws. Is that your marriage?

Maybe you're more like Sally and I used to be—neither hot nor cold. While deeply committed to each other, in reality, we were disconnected from each other. Our marriage was lukewarm, stale, and lifeless.

Young J. D. and Alecia were still in love—they hadn't taken that slide down into marital mediocrity—and didn't want to. Was it inevitable that they would?

Wherever you or I find ourselves on the scale of marital conflict, the crucial issue we have to address is the same. Jeremiah spelled it out thousands of years ago:

> "For My people have committed two evils:
> They have forsaken Me, the fountain of living waters,
> And hewn themselves cisterns—broken cisterns that can hold no water."[1]

Cracked cisterns

The ancient Palestinians commonly excavated cisterns out of limestone rocks. They would haul water to fill them or trap rainwater. It was a logical way to survive in their dry climate. But what would you think of them if they had easy access to a gushing, sweet spring—and yet still chose to depend on the water stagnating in their cisterns? Worse yet, sometimes those cisterns cracked, and the water leaked out. Can you imagine a dusty, thirsty Palestinian farmer sucking up the puddles from the bottom of his cracked cistern, when just a short distance away was a green oasis with gurgling streams flowing into clear, deep pools? Wouldn't you wonder if something besides his cistern was cracked?

What is so obvious in this illustration is not obvious in our everyday lives, and yet we all do it. God is our only Source of love, life, and joy, yet every one of us tends to turn from Him to substitutes. We chart our own course, try to solve our own problems, and attempt to create our own oases.

That's what was happening with Stan and Susan. They were both thirsty for love—and they were both trying to extract it from broken cisterns. The result was that neither of them was able to bring sweet water into their marriage.

Now you may be saying, "I understand, Jim, that *Stan* was chasing the

---

1. Jeremiah 2:13.

broken cisterns of the world—but how can you say that about Susan? She was trying to live a godly life. Surely you aren't saying that her church attendance, reforms, and outreach were broken cisterns, are you?"

That's exactly what I'm saying, and Susan was the hardest person to convince. Stan knew that what he was doing was wrong. But Susan was doing so many things right! The problem was that those right things all became *substitutes* for the Fountain of living waters. Her religiosity, her "churchianity," her "reformianity" were all *her* doing. She was still the one in charge. How do I know that? Because James 3:14, 15 says that "if you have bitter envy and self-seeking in your hearts, do not boast and lie against the truth. This wisdom does not descend *from above,* but is earthly, sensual, demonic" (emphasis supplied).

If Susan had been drinking from the fountain of God, she would have the "wisdom that is from above [that] is first pure, then peaceable, gentle, willing to yield, full of mercy and good fruits, without partiality and without hypocrisy."[2]

Think about it. What would a marriage be like if that verse truly described both husband and wife? Can you imagine what your home would be like if both you and your spouse demonstrated the fruits of the Spirit—love, joy, peace, gentleness, patience, forbearance, self-control, and faith—when things don't go your way? Wouldn't you find that irresistible?

Although Stan and Susan were opposites in many ways, they both needed the same prescription: a return to God, the Fountain of living waters! You see, God has all the wisdom, power, and resources Stan and Susan need to fix their marriage. He knows how to balance their imbalances. He has the creative power to subdue Stan's selfishness. He has the wisdom to correct Susan's judgmentalism. More than that, He can infuse life into them. Their marriage might be a desert, but if Stan and Susan allow God to irrigate it with His Spirit, it will become a lush, irresistible garden! But in order for God to accomplish this, He must be allowed to be God.

Principle one

Principle one is very simple: " ' "You shall love the LORD your God with all your heart, with all your soul, with all your strength, and with all your mind." ' "[3] He is the great I AM. He was. He is. And He is there for you. He takes a personal interest in you and me.

Loving God means that He—not your spouse or anything else—becomes your Source of joy and love. You accept the love that comes from your spouse as an overflow of God's love for you. Your love for your spouse is

---

2. Verse 17.
3. Luke 10:27.

God's love flowing through you. This frees you to release your spouse from responsibility for your emotions, expectations, and actions. God becomes your Counselor and Guide, and you are accountable to Him for the way you think, feel, and behave.

You see, God has promised to supply all our needs. He—not your spouse—is the real Source of love and joy. In the Garden, Adam lost sight of this. When faced with separation from Eve, because of her sin, he chose Eve over God. He forgot that God was the One who supplied his needs—and that God was not dependent on Eve to accomplish that for him.

Like Adam, we often forget the One who supplies our needs, and we step out of God's will. We try to meet our own needs or we try to "make" our mates meet our needs—and we throw temper tantrums or pine away in despair when they don't. But if we would love God supremely, He has a thousand ways to care for us that we don't understand.

Does this mean that God becomes a replacement for your spouse? Not at all! Rather, allowing God to be God equips you to connect deeply with your spouse. God created Adam in such a way that even in a perfect state Adam was still lonely. Why? Because God had something in mind for him—something that would complement him. The One who declared in the Garden of Eden, " 'It is not good that the man should be alone' " is also the One who decided, " 'I will make him a helper comparable to him.' "[4]

Do you think Adam and Eve had a dull evening that first Friday night when God brought them together in Eden? Not in the least. Their marriage sparkled! It was fresh, vibrant, and fulfilling! That's how God designed it to be. His involvement doesn't diminish our delight. It increases it! Too often we think of God as the ultimate wet blanket, but nothing could be further from the truth. That's why husbands and wives need to go to Him to know how to respond to each other.

Engaging with God

"Stan and Susan," I counseled, "the first step is simple. For the next ninety days, I don't want you to say anything or do anything until you filter it through God. He is your wisdom. You are to become 'swift to hear His voice, slow to speak your own words, and slow to wrath.'[5]

"God has given you a conscience, and in the next ninety days, I want you to educate and reactivate your consciences so that the lightest whisper of Jesus will move your soul, your words, your feelings, and your actions. Loving Him means obeying His directions in accordance with His Word. Don't

---

4. Genesis 2:18.
5. James 1:19, personal paraphrase.

fear this, because you can never outlove God. He will give you far more than you can ever give Him.

"Begin by spending time with God at the beginning and the end of the day. Spending time with God, contemplating the principles of His Word as they are impressed upon your hearts by the Holy Spirit will educate and reactivate your consciences. God wants to engage you to compare His ways with your ways, His character with your characters, His manner of approaching life with your own. And then He will point out the steps for you to take to come nearer His ideal."

Susan interjected, "Jim, I already do that. I spend an hour studying and praying almost every morning—but it doesn't change much in my life!"

"It used to be that way for me, too, Susan. I spent quality time with God's Word, but still had no power over my irritation with Sally. It took me a while to realize that I was approaching God's Word to acquire information or to satisfy my curiosity or to prove myself right and someone else wrong. I didn't realize how arrogant my approach was, how much I resembled the Pharisee who prayed aloud, ' "God, I thank You that I am not like other men." ' I had to learn to approach my quiet time with God with the attitude of the publican: ' "God, be merciful to me a sinner!" '[6] As I began to realize how desperately I needed God's help, my quiet time changed. I began to grasp that the mighty God of the universe takes a personal interest in me, and I began to hear His voice speaking to my own heart through the pages of His Word. I began to see where my attitudes needed to change and that God was always there to help me. Does that make sense to you, Susan?"

I paused, and the phone lines were silent except for a few quiet sniffles coming from Susan. "I think I know what you're saying, Jim. I've often heard you preach about that, and your books all talk about it. But I guess that at some deep level, I'm not sure God is really there for me."

"That's where faith comes in, Susan. It's choosing to venture on what God promises rather than what we've experienced. If you will experiment with relinquishing control to God, you will taste for yourself that He truly is there for you.

"As you move into your day, maintain a consciousness of God's presence with you and keep your ear tuned to hear His directions—how to implement the principles you studied in the morning. Then respond when He calls. That's how you become a doer of the Word and not a hearer only.

"Then at the end of the day, you take time to reflect on how things went, sort of like the way a football team replays Sunday night's game on Monday morning. What went well and what went wrong? Did God call to

---

6. Luke 18:11, 13.

my conscience? Did I listen to Him or ignore Him? I like to slip into the tub, take a sauna, or go for a walk, and just let my mind quiet down as I process the day. In this way, you engage with God and learn to turn to Him instead of to your broken cisterns.

"Stan," I continued, turning the conversation to him. "I know you aren't in the habit of having a devotional life, but you, too, need to carve out time for God. As it is now, you're like a football player running out onto the field without consulting the coach—and then wondering why you keep fumbling the ball. If you really want to give your marriage a chance, you'll have to get up in time to huddle with your Coach—that's another way I refer to God—and listen to His directions. You aren't accustomed to reading the Bible or praying, so it will seem unnatural to you at first. But in time, it will become one of your favorite times of the day, because it will make such a difference for the better in your life and marriage."

"But, Jim, I work for a living! I don't have time for all that. Am I supposed to quit my job and become a monk?"

"Stan, what time do you usually get off work?"

"Oh, between six and seven in the evening."

"And what time do you go to bed?"

"Around midnight."

"How do you customarily spend your evenings?"

There was a long pause. "I get the point, Jim. I'm going to have to prune some things out of my day to make room for God."

"Stan, that's turning from your broken cisterns and returning to God. You can't see it now, but you will taste something better than you've ever had before."

Skeptical and scared

Susan was skeptical, but Stan was scared to death. Deep down, he believed life would degenerate into a mere stale existence if he didn't live it his way. How could someone so accustomed to the pleasures of this world ever be satisfied with a life of pure motives and simple joys? Stan couldn't see it, but he was willing to try. For the sake of his children and the shallow love he possessed for his wife, he was willing to try to live this way—for ninety days at least. And try it they did—both Stan and Susan.

When Stan was tempted to complain about Susan's cooking, God broke into his thoughts reminding him of a principle he had read: "Do all things without complaining or disputing."[7] Out of love for God, Stan would eat his meal quietly and thank Susan for her efforts. When Susan was tempted

---
7. Philippians 2:14.

to tell Stan what he ought to be doing, God would remind her to "let your speech always be with grace, seasoned with salt, that you may know how you ought to answer each one."[8] They began to learn that circumstances did not have to control them—that they could modify their knee-jerk reactions to each other.

Stumbling in old ruts

Yes, it was very awkward at first, and their execution was less than flawless in that ninety-day trial. In fact, some of their stumbles were very painful. That's not surprising! We all are prone to fall back into our old ruts. For Stan and Susan, their stumbling block was the "blame game"!

Susan, the early bird, was having her usual quiet time, but Stan was oversleeping. As the minutes ticked by, Susan felt her agitation increasing. "He's supposed to be up spending time with God. If he doesn't, he probably won't be nice to me, and everything will go back to the way it used to be." The longer Susan sat there trying to read and pray, the more irritated she felt—until when Stan finally got up and came out of the bedroom, she was quite worked up. "You sure overslept! Now you don't have much time before you're supposed to be at work."

Stan was instantly irritated. "Mind your own business!" he snapped. He had been planning to spend what little time he had finding a Scripture thought for the day, but suddenly he had no inclination to do that. "I'm going to work early today," and he headed to the kitchen where he opened the refrigerator and stood staring at the contents. "Why can't we ever have some decent food around here? Everything always has to be so *&%#*&% 'healthy'!" Stan grabbed the milk and slammed the refrigerator door. Fixing himself a bowl of cereal, he snatched a spoon and dashed out the door to work.

Both Susan and Stan sensed they were blowing it. Each tried to cry out to God in their own minds, but their emotions were riled up and that still, small Voice seemed imperceptible. Susan tried to begin her day, but all morning long her mind kept rehearsing the same troubled thoughts she had felt earlier. Stan just put the whole situation out of his mind and refused to think about it.

When Stan came home that night, Susan's agitation and his irritation clashed all over again, and the verbal volleys escalated. As Stan retreated to his Internet haven, Susan got in the last punch, "You're not keeping your end of the bargain, Stan. It's not going to work if you don't. Jim said so!"

Stan slammed the door muttering to himself, "If Susan wasn't such a nag and so 'holy,' a guy might be inclined to be nice to her."

---

8. Colossians 4:6.

Accountability time

The next evening was our weekly phone-counseling appointment. "Well, how are you two doing?" I asked.

Silence.

"Stan, on a scale of one to ten, how would you rate the way things are going?"

"Maybe a four or a five."

"What would you say, Susan?"

"I'd give it maybe a one."

"A one!" objected Stan. "It's not that bad, Susan! You're always exaggerating."

"Maybe it's not that bad for you, but it is for me. You always gloss over things, because you don't want to deal with them!"

"Wait a minute, you two," I interrupted. "What did you both agree to do in all your interactions with each other?"

"We're supposed to filter everything through God," Susan quickly replied. "But Stan hasn't been spending his time with God, and he's just like he's always been."

Stan fired back, "Well, Susan spends her time with God, all right—but it doesn't do any good. She's still a crank to live with."

"Wait a minute, wait a minute! Stan, I'm not interested in your evaluation of Susan. What I want to know from you is have you been filtering all *your* thoughts, words, and actions through God?"

Stan was a bit deflated. "Well, no. I guess I haven't."

"That's OK, Stan. You've stumbled. But the question to be answered now is, Are you willing to get back up?"

Stan wasn't so sure he wanted to pick it up again, but after he realized that his other option was losing his family, he made up his mind. "OK, I'll give it another try."

"What about you, Susan? I don't want to hear your complaints about Stan. I just want you to answer the same question: have you been filtering your thoughts, words, and actions through God?"

"Well I was trying, but something must have gone wrong somewhere. I guess not, Jim. But sometimes the thoughts and feelings get so overpowering, I don't know what to do with them." Her voice grew strained, and I thought she must be crying.

"We'll get to that in a moment," I assured her. "First, I want to know, are you willing to get back on the program?"

She paused, and I could hear her sniffling and blowing her nose. "Yes, I am. I'm sorry for nagging you, Stan."

I could sense that Susan wasn't the only one struggling with tears. Stan managed to choke out, "I'm sorry for being insensitive to you, Susan. I really do want our marriage to work."

"Now, I don't want you two to become discouraged. Proverbs chapter twenty-four, verse sixteen says that 'a righteous man may fall seven times, And rise again.' So you've stumbled and gone back to the old ways. God's not here to kick you around. He just wants you to take His hand, get back up, and try again."

"Jim, I didn't want to stumble," Stan insisted. "It just sort of happened. I woke up with every good intention of filtering everything through God, but that went out the window as soon as Susan made her comment. At that point, I could see only red, and everything else just seemed to happen automatically."

"Me, too, Jim," Susan added. "I mean, I was sitting right there having my quiet time when these strong feelings of agitation came over me. I tried to surrender them to God, and I wanted to say something nice to Stan when he came out of the bedroom, but when I opened my mouth, it just didn't come out right. And I found myself going down into the same old miserable rut with him. I didn't want to, but I did."

Why?

Have you ever been in the situation Susan and Stan described? We all have, haven't we? We see what is right, and we want to do it—but we find ourselves doing what is wrong. Then we're tempted either to defend what we did, blame someone else or our circumstances, or give up in discouragement. But God asks us simply to acknowledge our shortcomings and face them.[9] In His hands, these failures can become stepping-stones to genuine freedom.

God wants us to understand what causes us to stumble. Isaiah says, "A deceived heart has turned him aside."[10] In other words, when Stan or Susan believe something that is not true, that misguided belief turns them aside from the path in which God is leading them. But often they can't discern that misguided belief, because it is such a part of them. As long as the misguided belief is undetected, they will be vulnerable to temptations in that area.

Most of us underestimate the power our belief system has over us—to our detriment. Jesus said, " 'According to your faith let it be to you.' "[11] Another word for "faith" is *belief*—according to your "belief" let it be to you. I don't believe that Jesus was referring in this text only to our doctrinal beliefs, although they have an important place. He was including everything

---

9. See Proverbs 28:13.
10. Isaiah 44:20.
11. Matthew 9:29.

we believe about ourselves, other people, the world around us, and God.

What we believe will dictate how we behave. Why? Because "as he thinks in his heart, so is he."[12] For example, if you are convinced that you can sleep *only* when you are wearing purple pajamas, you will likely get a bit upset when your purple pajamas don't get through the laundry before bedtime. Is that an irrational belief? Of course, it is—but if you believed it, it wouldn't seem irrational *to you*. Many of the beliefs people rely on are just as irrational when compared with the Word of God—and yet we operate on them automatically, without stopping to think about them, because they are as familiar to us as our favorite old slippers—just waiting for us to slip comfortably into them. The problem is that these misguided beliefs are the source of much of our emotional turmoil and destructive behavior.

A simple illustration will make this clear. Have you ever been by a field of sunflowers? What you notice first is their cheerful faces, turning toward the sun. What are less evident are the leaves and stems that support the flowers and the system of roots hidden beneath the soil that nourish the entire plant.

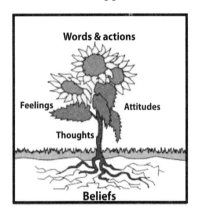

Every one of us has a belief system rooted in our minds. Out of that belief system stems a constant flow of thoughts that feed our feelings, attitudes, words, and actions. Every event we have experienced from our mother's womb until now—whether pleasurable or painful—has had an impact on our belief system. Satan uses the experiences of life to deceive our hearts and to misguide our beliefs. He knows that by doing so he can turn us aside from God's path and lead us to destruction—unless we engage with God.

Recap

Let's get into Stan's and Susan's heads that morning. Susan was reading the Bible, but the flow of her thoughts—arising from her belief system—was doing something else that she didn't recognize. How might she have known that? By her rising feelings of agitation. Our negative emotions are excellent clues to identifying our misguided beliefs. Instead of discounting them, it's best to acknowledge them and ask God to show us what is driving them and what to do with them.

---

12. Proverbs 23:7.

The Fountain of Irresistibility

Susan's misguided beliefs were telling her something like this: *If Stan isn't connected to God, he isn't going to treat me right, and that's just awful. It's intolerable! I can't stand it if he is not the kind of husband he should be. I have a right to demand that Stan treat me and our children with love and thoughtfulness. In fact, since he married me, he owes me love. I have a right to be angry if he doesn't meet my expectations.*

Meanwhile, Stan had just woken up. He rolled over and looked at the clock. Rubbing his bleary eyes, he shook his head in disbelief. *I overslept a whole hour,* he thought. *I didn't even hear the alarm go off or Susan get out of bed. And I promised Jim I would try to spend an hour every morning with God. It's impossible. I just can't get out of bed in the morning. Why even try? Now I'll have to face Susan. She'll be quick to point out my failure, and I just can't stand that! There can't be anything more miserable than being married to a perfect saint—especially one that has no trouble getting up with the birds and staying on a schedule. I'm not sure this new program is worth the struggle!*

With these kinds of thoughts spinning around in their heads, it's no wonder Susan felt agitated and Stan felt attacked when he came out of the bedroom! Please note that neither of them was fully aware of these thoughts—they didn't think these things in words. Their thoughts consisted more of mental images that translated into powerful emotions.

Both Susan and Stan needed to step back from the situation, take a deep breath, and let their emotions calm down. God had a solution for them. " 'Come now, and let us reason together,' Says the Lord."[13] " 'You shall know the truth, and the truth shall make you free.' "[14]

The way out

God wants to work with Stan's and Susan's minds; He wants to expose their misguided beliefs and replace them with truth. He's not concerned only with changing what they *do*—He wants to deal with the reason *why* they do what they do. Both Stan and Susan need to ask themselves: "*Why* did I react the way that I did? *Why* do these circumstances have such a grip on me?" Stan needs to think about how he responded to Susan. "*Why* did I treat her like my worst enemy?" Susan needs to stop and ask herself, "*Why* did I get so angry when Stan didn't get up for his quiet time?"

This kind of introspection would open the door for God to reveal to them their misguided beliefs—and that is the key for real, lasting change. It took some time and reflection, as well as feedback from Sally and me, to help Susan and Stan identify their misguided beliefs. Their time alone with

---

13. Isaiah 1:18.
14. John 8:32.

God became very relevant to them as they searched His Word for clues. Susan was amazed at what she found. She outlined it like this:

Misguided Beliefs	Truth
1. It's awful that Stan doesn't treat me the way he ought to treat me.	1. It would be nice if Stan treated me well, but God has promised to provide all of my needs—including my need for love and acceptance—according to His riches in glory.[15] I'm not dependent on Stan's behavior to be a happy wife.[16]
2. I can't stand it that Stan is not the kind of husband he should be.	2. I would like very much to have a close and satisfying relationship with Stan, but it is not absolutely essential to my well-being. Through Christ, I can rise above the disappointments that are inevitable in a close relationship and pray for Stan through them.[17]
3. I have a right to demand that Stan treat me well. He owes me love.	3. It would be wonderful to be loved by Stan, but it is not essential for my happiness. Furthermore, love only flourishes in freedom. It cannot be demanded. When I demand that Stan love me, I create an environment hostile to love. God can fill my need for love and acceptance, and then His love through me can spill over onto Stan, freeing him to love me if he chooses to do so.[18]

---

15. See Philippians 4:19.
16. See Isaiah 54:5.
17. See Psalm 62:5.
18. See 1 John 4:18.

4. I have a right to be angry if Stan doesn't do it.	4. God doesn't want me to be angry over what I cannot change. It ends up hurting more than helping.[19] Instead, I need to see Stan as he can be in Jesus and ask God to show me how I can bless him rather than nag him.[20]

As Susan began this process, she made a disconcerting discovery. "Jim, I've known all these texts for years. I've even memorized most of them. But that knowledge didn't change how I have treated Stan. How can that be?"

"Susan, you're not alone. Most people live with an abyss between what they know intellectually and what they practice. It's as though the soil around the roots of their beliefs has been fertilized with a lot of precious truth, but they don't draw it in, and so they continue to do automatically what they have always done.

"For example, too many of us have a deep-seated misconception that God is not real and that He is not actively involved in our lives. We know in our heads that He is there, but the part of us that engages in our day-to-day actions operates as though He were not. Instead of consulting with Him, we call our own shots. There is an incongruity between what we intellectually know to be true and what we really believe. It's the difference between an intellectual assent to facts and a living faith."

Susan was catching on. "That's so true, Jim. The other day I read, 'Be content with such things as you have. For He Himself has said, "I will never leave you nor forsake you." '[21] I know that's true, and yet so often my actions have very clearly shouted that I am not content. I'm beginning to understand that I need to act on that truth in spite of my feelings and old habit patterns until it replaces my old ways."

"You're right, Susan. That's why we need to take time to wait on God. God wants not only to fertilize the soil of our brains with truth as we study

---

19. See Psalm 37:8.
20. See Philippians 4:8; Romans 12:17.
21. Hebrews 13:5.

His Word, but He also longs to whisper to us, throughout the day, the application of that truth so that it controls our responses to life. As we cooperate with this process, our emotions and actions become pure, peaceable, and gentle. The stream of our thoughts nurtures a vibrant, truth-filled, living faith. This is what David was referring to when he wrote, 'Behold, You desire truth in the inward parts, And in the hidden part You will make me to know wisdom.' "[22]

Surprise!

Stan engaged in the learning process, too, and made a tremendous discovery. Learning to walk with God is not the end of good living—it's only the beginning! Stan found an inner freedom he had never before tasted, and he wanted more. Here's part of what he discovered.

Misguided Beliefs	**Truth**
1. It's impossible. I just can't get out of bed in the morning. Why even try?	1. "I can do all things through Christ who strengthens me."[23] If I knew I was going to be rewarded with $10,000 for getting out of bed, I'd find a way to do it. God is offering me the keys to restore irresistible love to my marriage, and that is priceless. I *can* learn to get out of bed on time.
2. Susan will be quick to point out my failure, and I just can't stand that!	2. I would like it if Susan didn't point out my stumbles as if she is my judge, but I can't control her responses to me. Why keep upsetting myself over something I can't change?[24]

---

22. Psalm 51:6.
23. Philippians 4:13.
24. See Romans 14:12; Proverbs 16:32.

3. There can't be anything more miserable than being married to a perfect saint.	3. There *is* something more miserable than being married to Susan—facing divorce from Susan. By God's grace, I can love her instead of fighting with her.[25]
4. I'm not sure this new program is worth the struggle!	4. My marriage and family are worth fighting for![26]

It works!

This process of quiet introspection with God—combined with filtering through Him all that they thought, said, or did in their interactions with each other—bore wonderful fruit. They connected with the Fountain of irresistibility, and His life and love began to flow through them. They discovered that God knows very well how to mend two broken hearts and open them to each other. The second principle I shared with Stan and Susan is an outgrowth of this first principle. It is so rewarding, I can hardly wait to tell you about it!

But first, let me encourage you that what worked for Stan and Susan will work for you too—whether you want to avoid divorce, add zest to your relationship, or stay in love.

Why wait? Go to the Fountain now. It's always flowing!

---

25. See Romans 5:5.
26. See Ephesians 5:28.

Study Questions for Chapter 2

1. Do you believe that without God you can do nothing?
2. Do you believe that God has forsaken you or your marriage?
3. Do you believe that God can—and will—guide you daily?
4. Do you see yourself in any of the scenarios described in this chapter?
5. Do you feel there is hope for your marriage?
6. Are you willing to enter into the first step as outlined in this chapter?
7. If not, are you willing to be made willing?
8. Do you recognize the misguided beliefs that rob you of your peace and joy?
9. Are you willing to examine these beliefs and filter them through God?
10. Is this step too scary to take?
11. Do you realize that the sure way to failure is to fail to try?
12. Are you willing to let God revitalize your marriage—beginning with you?
13. If so, are you prepared to try His program instead of your own?

CHAPTER 3

Becoming Irresistible

"The Son of Man did not come to be served, but to serve."
—Matthew 20:28

I'll never forget that November afternoon talking with J. D. and Alecia. The temperature outside was dropping, and snow flurries swirled around our cabin. But it was warm inside! And not just because of the woodstove radiating heat in the corner of the living room!

J. D. and Alecia were cozied up on the couch, and as I asked them what questions they had for me, they looked at each other. "Would you like to go first?" J. D. asked Alecia with a twinkle in his eye.

"That's all right. Why don't you start?" Alecia deferred to him sweetly.

As we got into the conversation, Alecia started to squirm in her seat just a bit. I didn't notice—but J. D. did! Momentarily distracted from what I was saying, he adjusted his position to make her more comfortable. A little later, J. D. got a dry tickle in his throat. Without any other cue, Alecia got up to get him a drink of water.

Principle two

J. D. and Alecia were tuned in to each other! Each was focused on the other and looked for opportunities to serve the other. That's the second principle in a nutshell. "You shall love your spouse as yourself."[1] When a husband and wife *both* focus on understanding each other's needs and watch for opportunities to minister to the other, their hearts will remain open and connected. Their unselfishness feeds a cycle of bonding that deepens and grows in spite of the trials and disappointments that are an inherent part of life in a fallen world. They remain irresistible to each other.

---

1. Luke 10:27, personal paraphrase.

"So then, Mr. Hohnberger, how do we stay in love?" Alecia's question was earnest and heartfelt. J. D.'s eyes told me that he shared Alecia's longing not to lose what they presently possessed—what everyone told them they would lose.

I shared with them the first principle—practical dependence on God—and then explained the second. "Find out what says 'I love you' to your spouse and then do it—daily! As long as both of you remain focused on each other, rather than what you're getting or not getting from the marriage, you will stay in love. As we've already discussed, the 'tingles' will likely diminish. You will both learn things about each other that are impossible for you to know now—and life will challenge and test you. But if you keep coming back to these two principles, your love will only grow in the crucible of life.

"As I've worked with scores of troubled marriages, I've observed that in almost every case the trouble boils down to one thing: 'You don't love me as you did at first.' When this moment comes—and it comes into most marriages either gradually or all at once—it can have devastating effects. But divorce, separation, or simply coexisting are *not* the only options!"

Alecia burst out, "Mr. Hohnberger, I just can't believe that could happen to us. Do things really change that much when a person gets married?"

Changes and challenges

"Yes," I admitted, "things do change when you get married. You now share the same home, the same room, and the same bed. You've got to work through such things as how you handle the finances, who empties the trash and makes the bed, differences in sexual needs, and a whole host of things that you can *talk about* before marriage but do not *experience* until you say, 'I do.' In addition, real life begins to press onto your shoulders. You've got to make a living. Other relationships need to be tended to. There are domestic tasks to manage. Children come along.

"The little crises of life, such as flat tires and clogged plumbing, seem like adventures to the two of you while the chemistry is high. But after a while, those same experiences are simply mundane nuisances, and the way your spouse approaches them may seem incomprehensible.

"In addition, the family you grew up in greatly influences how you approach your role as a spouse and your expectations of your partner. Most people slip into patterns of relating to their husband or wife based on what they observed in their parents. If their parents were good communicators, they will tend to be the same. If they grew up in a combative atmosphere, they will tend to expect a fight.

"At the same time, because of the commitment you and your spouse have made, you start feeling safe. It becomes natural to stop putting your best foot forward and to 'just be yourself.' And yet, you're surprised when you see your mate doing the same thing. You assumed he or she would always be the way you knew him or her to be while you were courting. And so, little irritations begin to creep in.

"Combine all these things with the false expectations our society has built up about love, and you have a surefire recipe for disillusionment. For example, many of us have been led to erroneously believe that happy, stable couples never argue, get angry, or disagree. That they are not dependent on one another. That both want sex equally. That they never feel lonely or bored and always know what the other wants. Modern love stories picture a couple saying 'I do' and then riding off into the sunset to live happily ever after. But that's not real life—or real love!

Camping catastrophe

"For example, one couple I knew were madly in love when they got married. In his eyes, she was the best thing that could ever have happened to him. As far as she was concerned, no other man could hold a candle to her Prince Charming. Their finances were limited, so as they planned their wedding, Larry asked Sheila if she liked camping. 'Oh, I love camping!' she replied enthusiastically.

"Warm memories of 'roughing it' with her family came to her mind. They would go to a fully equipped campground. You know, the ones that have bathrooms with flush toilets and hot showers, paved roads and bike trails, picnic tables, and big fire rings with grills. Her father always rented a U-Haul trailer to carry all their gear. He would set up a wall tent complete with cots, clothes racks, and a stove to warm up those cool mornings and evenings. They cooked their meals over a three-burner propane grill and always planned their activities near other people. Wild animals lurk in the woods, you know. Sheila didn't know there was any other way to camp.

"So when Larry suggested, 'Why don't we go camping in the redwoods for our honeymoon?' Sheila immediately responded, 'I'd love that!' It never occurred to either of them to compare their ideas of camping!

"Larry planned to set up their camp before the wedding so that everything would be ready and just perfect for his new bride. He talked to some of the old timers in the area who told him about a secluded area nobody frequented. He went searching with his 4 x 4 pickup until he found the ideal place—a small clearing near a gurgling brook surrounded by redwoods and cedars with lots of deer, elk, and bear tracks in the soft dirt. It was quiet, private—and free! He set up his two-man backpacking tent, zipped two sleeping bags together, and laid them on a couple of foam pads. Using a few choice stones from the nearby stream, he built a small fire ring and collected a nice pile of firewood. Then he stood back and wondered, *What else could I do to make this really special for Sheila? Hmm. I know! She'd like something to sit on while she cooks over the fire. There's a log that will do.* Larry rolled it over, trimmed off the branches, and even peeled off some of the bark. He placed it so it wouldn't roll around and then thought, *This is perfect! She is going to be so surprised!*

"He didn't realize what an understatement that was! As Larry and Sheila bounced slowly up the old logging road, Sheila grew quieter and quieter. Finally, they arrived. 'We're here!' Larry announced excitedly.

" 'We are?' Sheila tried to contain her mounting consternation. 'Where's the campground?'

" 'Campground? I never go to campgrounds. They're too noisy. Too many people, and you have to pay for them.'

" 'But where's the bathroom?'

" 'Bathroom? Just pick your tree.'

" 'And I'll need a shower—I can't go a day without a shower—especially on my honeymoon!'

" 'Well, there's plenty of running water in the creek.'

"Sheila was horrified, while Larry was mystified. Needless to say, those two had a rather rocky start. But their surprises didn't end with the honeymoon. Sheila had grown up in a home where both parents worked outside the home, and her father took responsibility for all the housework and cooking. Sheila was his pride and joy, and he didn't want her to be saddled with too much responsibility. So she never learned how to clean a house. Baking cookies and doughnuts were the limits of her culinary expertise. On the other hand, a stay-at-home mother who did all the domestic chores raised Larry. It never crossed his father's mind to lift a finger to help her. I don't have to spell out the conflict Larry and Sheila experienced working through that one!

"Both of them had to make some rather big adjustments in their expectations and anticipated roles. Hopefully, you—Alecia and J. D.—won't face surprises quite that drastic, but you will learn things about each other you don't expect now. And not every discovery will seem delightful to you.

"That's when you are the most vulnerable to losing your first love. God has some simple, yet comprehensive counsel that will help you hold on to that first love—or to find it again if you have let it slip. The Lord says, 'Yet there is one thing wrong. You don't love Me as at first. Think about those times of your first love—how different it is now. Turn back to Me again and work as you did before.'[2]

Universal prescription

"God admonishes us to *think* about those times of our 'first love.' No, you can't necessarily reactivate the love cocktail that sends tingles up and down your spine—but there are things you did *automatically* when under the influence of that love cocktail that you can continue to do *intentionally*. Some of these things are

- focus on the other person;
- prioritize your life, your time, and your activities around your spouse;
- desire to please your spouse;
- give your spouse your time and attention;
- touch each other affectionately;
- talk about your future together in positive terms;
- share dreams, ideas, and goals;
- laugh together;
- play together;
- support each other through difficult circumstances;
- give each other the benefit of the doubt;
- and work together to resolve differences.

"Isn't that how you two treat each other now?" I asked J. D. and Alecia. They looked at each other, and smiles wreathed their faces. "We do—and it's not hard. It just seems to happen naturally. That's why it's hard to imagine it could ever be different. How could we 'fall out of love'?"

"Well," I answered, "combined with the other factors we've already talked about, many couples simply stop doing what they used to do so easily, so naturally. It's not that those things are no longer a priority. They simply become less of a priority. You begin to love each other in conjunction with many other things. Soon those other things can steal your time and affections, and your first love slides into second, third, or fourth place. Men begin to spend more time in business and employment. They put more interest into sports, news, and politics. For some, it may even be the church—giving Bible studies or doing outreach and evangelism. Many men become more fascinated with the Internet than with their wives.

---

2. Revelation 2:4, 5, personal paraphrase.

"The same can happen in other ways for the wife. Her husband doesn't seem quite as irresistible as he once did. To fill the gap, she spends more time on the telephone, with the children, or at the shopping mall. Perhaps it's her parents or her best friend that now takes that first place in her life.

"Whatever it is that steals your first love, the prescription is the same. 'Turn back to Me again and work as you did before.'[3] It's not complicated, complex, or confusing. It's quite simple! The attitude of *I'm here for you—period* must resurface and take precedence in your everyday life. It isn't *trying* to get your mate to become irresistible—it's *becoming* irresistible to him or her by drawing life, love, and wisdom from God and living it out with your spouse under His direction.

"Underlying this attitude is a determination that the negative things that arise in your life or relationship will not destroy your love for one another. You must begin to see irritations as opportunities to understand your own blind spots and to grow. That attitude will also lead you to fight your own innate tendency to selfishness.

"Above all else, listen to God whispering to your heart how to serve one another. Here is where the first two principles tie in with each other. God is your ever-present Helper, and as you become sensitive to His presence with you, and as you filter all you say and do through Him, He will impress on your conscience how to touch the heart of your loved one in the things you do and say."

J. D. and Alecia liked that prescription! It fit them to a *T*. I didn't have to suggest a ninety-day program to them because they were already on it! They wanted to make it a way of life—a journey that would take them deeper and still deeper into genuine, lasting, intentional love.

Losing game or winning team?

Unfortunately, Stan and Susan didn't feel that way. When I explained step two, they were both silent. It sounded like a losing game to them.

"Stan, think back to the time you won Susan's heart. What did you do?"

"Oh, Jim. That was eons ago. I'm not sure what I did."

"How about you, Susan? Can you remember what you did that opened up Stan's heart?"

"Yeah, I can remember. I dressed the way I shouldn't. I cooked him food I shouldn't have cooked. And I was too physical with him. I'm sorry, Jim, but I can't go back to all that! My conscience won't let me."

"I'm not asking you to violate biblical principle or to do anything im-

---

3. Verse 5, personal paraphrase.

moral, Susan. Many couples get hung up on lust—and that's not what we're after. But there must have been some other things you did that didn't infringe on principle. Can you think of any of those things?"

Silence.

"No, Jim. I can't."

Practical assignment

"OK, here's this week's assignment for both of you. Take a 3 x 5 card and spend some time thinking about what the other did for you that opened your heart to him or her. Susan, I want you to write down three things that Stan could do for you that say 'I love you.' Stan, you do the same. Write down three things that Susan could do for you that say 'I love you.' Then exchange cards. This is Tuesday afternoon. How soon do you think you could do this?"

"I'll do it tonight," Stan replied.

"What about you, Susan?"

There was a long pause.

"If I do that, Jim, do I have to go back home?" Susan's voice quavered, and I could sense the immense emotional turmoil she was experiencing. It must have felt like volunteering to throw herself back into a gooey quagmire of quicksand, when she had just extricated herself from it. Her emotions were already settling into the idea of divorcing Stan and moving on. How could she open herself to hope—only to be devastated once more? My heart went out to this poor woman. What a choice!

"Susan, I'm not telling you what you have to do. That is between you and God. I'm simply giving you my recommendations. The best possibility your marriage has is for both you and Stan to engage in this two-step process, and since Stan says he's willing to get on board, you really need to be home in order to fully give it a chance. Does that make sense to you?"

By this time, Susan was sobbing. She choked out, "Yes, it makes sense. It's just so hard. I don't know if I can handle trying again."

Stan had been quiet, but now he spoke. "Susan, I don't blame you for feeling the way you do. I'm ashamed of the way I've treated you. I know I've hurt you deeply. I'm more sorry than you can know." He got choked up and couldn't speak for a moment. "I've hurt our children, and I've pushed you away. But I really don't want to lose you. I think our marriage is worth fighting for. Please give it a try for ninety days. If you don't see real change after that and you want to leave, I won't ask you to stay."

The phone was silent now except for the sounds of the two of them crying. I was praying fervently. Finally I asked, "Susan, what is God saying to you right now?"

More sobs. "I need to go home to Stan . . ." She couldn't say anymore for a moment. "Stan, I'll pack up tomorrow and be home by the following night! I'll have my card ready for you when I get there."

Stan let out a deep breath. "Oh, sweetheart! Thank you! By God's grace, I'll make you glad you made this decision."

I closed the conversation with one more recommendation. "There are a lot of well-meaning people that will want to give the two of you advice or sympathy. Their good intentions can amount to a lot of confusion. To give this program the best shot, I ask that you not confide in anyone else during the ninety days. Just ask them to pray for you."

They both agreed, and we said Goodbye. I thought of Stan and Susan and prayed for them often as the week went by. Would they follow through? Would Susan go home? Would she be glad she did? When they called at the appointed time, I was eager to hear their report.

To my amazement and joy, both of them were following the plan. That first week back together had been a real roller coaster. They had experienced both successes and fumbles as they began implementing the two principles: making God their Guide and focusing on serving each other. But they were hanging in there and seeing more hope than they had for years.

They had given each other their list of three requests, and we took some time to talk about them.

Susan's card

Here is what Susan had written on her card:

1. Come home on time and play with the children.
2. Work out with me three evenings a week.
3. Play miniature golf and take me out to eat twice a week.

Susan longed for Stan to spend time with her and the children. For her, this meant Stan would let Susan know what time he'd be home—and arrive at his stated time with a smile on his face. Instead of plopping down in front of the TV and grabbing the newspaper, he would play with the children. Susan loved to exercise, and Stan didn't. But he would work out with her three evenings a week, because she loved his companionship. Twice a week, Susan's aunt would babysit the children while Stan took Susan out to play miniature golf. Afterward, they would go to a quiet restaurant and talk about whatever was on their hearts. If Susan wanted to go for a walk, Stan wouldn't get on the Internet.

Stan realized that his attitude made a big difference in how he implemented these things. If he went through all the right motions but had a sour disposition, it would be counterproductive. "Jim," he confided, "this feels so unnatural. I feel like I'm playing a game and just going through the motions. Sometimes I'm not sure what to do—even knowing the three things on her card."

God's whisperings

"This is where you will find God's personal presence very practical, Stan," I told him. "God promises that 'your ears shall hear a word behind you, saying, "This is the way, walk in it." '[4] As you learn to be 'swift to hear' God's still, small Voice and 'slow to speak'[5] your own words and do your own thing, God's Spirit will tailor your thoughts and actions so that Susan sees a new you, one who is drinking from the Fountain of life and allowing the fruits of the Spirit—love, joy, peace, patience, kindness, goodness, faithfulness, and self-control—to flow through him. This is God's blueprint for re-establishing hope in Susan's heart that your marriage can work."[6]

"I know," Stan replied. "I've listened to you talk about these things in your sermons, Jim. But sometimes it gets pretty confusing. How do I recognize God's whisperings?"

Susan interjected, "I'm kind of struggling with the same thing, Jim—in spite of the fact I've been a Christian for a lot of years. How do you sort out in your mind what is coming from God and what is just your own stuff?"

"It's quite simple. When a thought or impression comes into my mind regarding my wife, I evaluate it according to biblical principles. If it is in accordance with Scripture and it leads me to deny myself and serve my wife, I conclude it is from God and act upon it.[7]

"For instance, Stan, if upon arriving home, you feel impressed to softly and gently hug and kiss your wife—do it! If you're reading the newspaper or are on the Internet, and you are pricked in your conscience to invite Susan to go for a walk—do it! After the evening meal, if you have a choice of either watching your favorite TV program or helping Susan do dishes, choose the course that denies self and puts her before you. While you're at work, if a thought comes to your mind to call your wife and say a word of encouragement—do it! This is allowing God to guide you. It's living the principles of His love

---

4. Isaiah 30:21.
5. James 1:19.
6. See Galatians 5:22, 23.
7. For a much broader explanation of understanding how God will personally direct you, see my book, *Escape to God*.

and His Word. It will open the flower of your wife's heart to you.

"Susan, when your husband has left for the day and you are on the phone and you sense God suggesting you make Stan his favorite meal—do it! If you know your husband likes a clean and orderly home, turn off the TV, pick up the house, iron his shirts, and enjoy the smile on his face and in his heart when he arrives home. If God whispers in your ear to take a refreshing shower and put on his favorite outfit before he returns home, do it! God knows what will open the heart of your man. He will stand by your side and whisper gently into your ear. If the suggestions that come to mind do not violate His Word, and if they put your husband first and yourself second, do follow them! Does that make sense?"

"Yes," Susan said thoughtfully. "It does."

Stan commented, "I think I know what you're saying, Jim. It sounds so easy when you talk about it."

"Well, you're right, Stan. None of this is complicated. It requires you only to say 'Yes' to God and 'No' to self. God will provide His grace, wisdom, and power. You are to respond to this saving grace as often as you recognize it. In doing so, you will do away with the old ways and develop a new way of living. That's why I say, give it ninety days. Not that your marriage will be perfected in ninety days, but that it will give you enough time to experience the liberating gospel in your marriage. Once you experience this freedom, I believe you'll be convinced to stay on God's program as a way of life.

Who will rule?

"Every couple I've met who has accepted this simple program now has an irresistible love for one another. Unfortunately, I run into some who say, 'I will not have this man rule over me.' Sadly, they don't seem to realize that either God or Satan ultimately rules over them. So, if they say 'No' to God, they are saying 'Yes' to Satan. Even God's church chose Caesar over Jesus. But that choice always ends in heartache and defeat. We kid ourselves thinking that *we* are in charge when, in essence, it is the spirit of the evil one moving through us."

Stan chuckled. "Sometimes I feel like such a phony! Sometimes I feel like laughing out loud at myself when I give Susan a compliment or hold her hand."

"I know what you mean, Stan, but don't give up. At the start, it may not seem real to you, but in time you'll reap good results, and it will become a way of life for you. For me, when I was willing to crucify my own self-rule and allow Christ to live in me,[8] my marriage was not only restored, but I also finally tasted the full gospel experience that so many of the famous hymns sing about."

Susan interjected, "I don't think you're a phony, Stan. Please don't stop what you're doing! I like it!" There was both warmth and pleading in her voice.

"Don't worry, Susan," Stan responded. "I may struggle at times, but I'm in this for the long haul, and I'm not going to give up. By the way, I like what you're doing too!"

I could practically see Susan blushing over the phone! "Oh yes, Susan, what was on Stan's card for you?" I asked.

She read me Stan's three requests, and I chuckled at their simplicity and frankness.

Stan's card

Here is what Stan had written:

1. Update your wardrobe.
2. Relax the menu.
3. Be my golf caddy.

With all her sincere intentions, Susan had taken dress "reform" to a bit of an extreme. She was an attractive woman, but she had adopted what I call "the covered wagon" look. Stan wasn't pushing for her to dress in miniskirts and plunging necklines, but he was asking her to update her clothing a bit. He also asked her not to impose her ideas of health reform on him so rigidly—and she agreed. If he didn't like tofu replacing his eggs, he would get the real thing. She would sweeten his pies with a little sugar instead of dates and make him buttermilk pancakes instead of buckwheat ones.

Stan loved to golf. In the early days of their courtship, Susan had gone with him and acted as his caddy. He had loved her energy and participation on the golf course. So, they agreed to arrange for a relative to babysit and spend every other Sunday morning together at the local golf course.

Sally and me

So, what's on your list? What's on your spouse's list? What would open your husband's or wife's heart to you? When God first brought this simple principle to my mind, I began to think about what had won Sally's heart in the first place. Fond memories flooded my mind of the two of us—young,

---

8. See Galatians 2:20.

footloose and fancy-free, riding my motorcycle out to High Cliff State Park in Wisconsin. We would climb the cliffs, find a favorite ledge to perch on, and then talk—for hours. Sally could talk about anything that was on her heart. I listened without editing her.

But by the time God brought this principle to my mind, we had moved to the wilderness of Montana; I didn't have a motorcycle; and we had children. In the wilderness, babysitters are pretty hard to find. Did that mean I couldn't work as before? Not at all! I instituted "swing time." Every day at noon I gave Sally my undivided attention for half an hour. More than that, instead of automatically tuning her out when she shared something with me, I began learning to listen to her. To this day, Sally loves it when I take her for a walk and we reminisce about good times of the past and share the joys and challenges of our present life. We invest time and energy into our relationship. By doing so, we are "working as we did before."

How about you?

What is your spouse's heart longing for? Do you know? Are you willing to explore it with God and begin to work as you did before? Here are some of the heart cries we hear from hurting spouses we counsel all over the world. Do you see yourself in any of these? Do you recognize your spouse?

- Please talk to me. I'd love to understand your perspective on things.
- Please get to the point. I want to understand you, but you wear me out with your excessive talking.
- I'd love to be treated as well as you treat others. You are available when they need you. You drop everything and throw yourself—your time, your heart, and your energy—into meeting their needs, while I wait forever.
- Your hobbies and other interests (sports, phone, friends, work) consume your time, and I don't fit into your life anymore. It's like having multiple wives. I must fit in where you let me, and I don't know where that is.
- Honey, if you'd just iron my shirts and hang them in the closet ready to wear, I'd be so happy. I like to be neat, and you never find time for what is important to me.
- You find plenty of time for your friends, their emotional needs, and giving sympathy to many. I need to be loved too. I'm not an ogre, you know. We need to talk, listen, and hear each other, and be willing to change.

- Honey, just allow me to spend some money—a reasonable amount—without harassing me or sending me on a guilt trip. You hold such a tight hand on the purse strings, I feel like I'm taking us to the poor house, buying some little thing. Trust me, so that I feel like you love me.
- Darling, can't we do something I like, even if you don't enjoy it? I'm always doing what you like to make you happy. Sometimes it would be fun to experience the reverse. I'd feel so loved if you would sacrifice in this way for me.

Apply our hearts to understanding

It's important to understand what your spouse wants. What says "I love you" to you may not strike an answering chord in your partner. Couples sometimes get frustrated because the husband tries to do for the wife what he wishes his wife would do for him. And the wife tries to do for her husband what she wishes he would do for her. Part of the reason is that men and women operate differently. They have different basic emotional needs, and it isn't natural for us to know automatically how those needs differ.

That's why God tells us to "apply your heart to understanding."[9] He wants us to understand each other. He created us differently—not to cause conflict, but so that husbands and wives could complement each other and be more together than either of them could be apart.

Paul succinctly summarized the differing needs of men and women in Ephesians 5:33, "Nevertheless let each one of you in particular so love his own wife as himself, and let the wife see that she respects her husband."

Women have a longing desire to be loved—unconditionally—for who they are. They want to be cherished, cared for, and understood. In the same way, men have a deep need to be respected—unconditionally—for who they are. They want to be admired, looked up to, and believed in.

When a husband loves his wife, she is motivated to respect him. When a wife respects her husband, he is motivated to love her. This cycle of meeting each other's basic needs is self-rewarding and energizing. In fact, it's great! All the gold in Alaska is not worth a marriage like that!

However, when a husband does not behave in ways that spell love to his wife, she tends to react by not respecting him. And when she behaves without respect, her husband tends to react without love. As you can see, they get into a vicious cycle of reacting to one another and not even understanding why. Dr. Emerson Eggerich calls this the "Crazy Cycle," and it can have devastating effects—alienating two hurting people and driving them farther and farther from each other. Stan and Susan were a classic—though somewhat

---

9. Proverbs 2:2.

extreme—case of this. But as they learned to connect with God for wisdom, power, and direction—and as they gained understanding of each other's heart cries—they stopped the cycle of craziness and entered a cycle of bonding their hearts together in genuine warmth and connection.

How is it with you? Do you relate more with J. D. and Alecia or with Stan and Susan? The ninety-day program is guaranteed to put you on the right track to repairing what is broken and preserving what is not. It works best if both you and your spouse enter into it, but don't get stuck in the trap so many people I meet trip over. "When my husband starts to love me, I'll get into the program." "When my wife gives me some respect, I'll think about it." So many couples stall, waiting for the other to take the first step. Why don't you be the one to take that first step today and begin to taste the fruit?

On the next page is a simple summary of the two principles with space for you to personalize and sign your commitment. You may wish to write your own commitment statement based on what God has spoken to your heart as you've contemplated these two principles. However you decide to do it, don't delay. Make the commitment today!

If you and your spouse both fill out this commitment and enter into it together, you will embark on a journey guaranteed to give you a little taste of heaven on earth. If your spouse is unwilling, unavailable, or otherwise not engaged, don't let that stop you! Enter into it yourself! Dare to become irresistible! Like Stan and Susan, you won't regret it!

Study Questions for Chapter 3

1. Would your spouse say he or she is first, second, third, fourth—or less—on your priority list in everyday living?
2. Do you know what says "I love you" to your spouse?
3. Spend a little time reminiscing about your courtship. What made you irresistible to your spouse?
4. Are you willing to "turn back" and renew your marriage?
5. Do you think the two-step process outlined in this chapter will work for you? If not, why not?
6. Are you willing to sign the ninety-day commitment?
7. Will God be able to say to you on the Judgment Day, "Well done, good and faithful spouse"?

The Ninety-Day Commitment

1. I will learn to listen to, and act on, the whisperings of God according to His principles.

2. I will learn what says "I love you" to my spouse and do it daily.

   Three things my husband could do that say "I love you" are:

   _____
   _____
   _____

   Three things my wife could do that say "I love you" are:

   _____
   _____
   _____

   Husband's signature: _____ Date: _____

   Wife's signature: _____ Date: _____

CHAPTER 4

Focused on Her

Husbands ... live with your wives in an understanding way ... and show her honor as a fellow heir of the grace of life, so that your prayers will not be hindered.

—*1 Peter 3:7, NASB*

[Note: This chapter is written especially for husbands, but wives are welcome to read along!]

"I just don't get it, Jim!" Bill's face was red, and he clenched and unclenched his fists as we walked out of the church and down the sidewalk. "I'm a successful attorney, and I bring home a good income. I built her a beautiful new home in one of the nicest neighborhoods in town. She has her pick of the furnishings and a brand-new sports car to boot. I give her everything she wants!" Bill kicked a stone into the gutter in frustration, then stopped and turned to face me. He was middle-aged with strikingly chiseled, tanned features and a well-toned physique evident even beneath his dress shirt.

"I've done my best to hold up godly standards in our home. I helped raise her kids in spite of the hell they put us through. I'm an elder at church, and everyone looks up to me—everyone except her, that is. She's been cold and distant to me for a long time, but I've done my best to be a good husband. And now this!

"I don't understand what she sees in Frank. He's sloppy, fat, and lazy. He tends the cash register in that convenience store down on the corner of Fifth and Everett, where he eats doughnuts and hot dogs all day. Once in a while, he slides the cash register drawer in and out for exercise. Oh—and I saw him get in his car the other day while I was pumping gas. It's a beat-up Oldsmobile from the eighties that leaves a cloud of smoke billowing behind it. I've never seen him dressed in anything but sweats and an old worn-out T-shirt. And yet, Barbara tells me she's in love with him! In love with him! When she has me! I just don't get it, Jim.

"I know Christians are supposed to be forgiving and all that, but sometimes I think about what I'd like to do to that guy if I met him in a dark alley some night. And what's wrong with Barbara? Why would she cheat on me with a guy like that? Is she trying to insult me—embarrass me? I just can't understand it!"

Bill clenched his fists again and snorted his aggravation. He was angry, for sure—and puzzled. But beneath his angry questioning, I could sense the hurt—the deep hurt of betrayal. *How could this have happened to him?*

We started walking back toward the church. I couldn't help but sympathize with Bill—knowing the tidal wave of emotion that would engulf me if my Sally were to do what his Barbara was doing. Memories of our early married life came flooding back. I had made some of the same mistakes I thought Bill was probably making. I had been successful in business, had given Sally all the comforts of life, and even a few of the luxuries. But I had missed what I sensed Bill was missing as well.

For the moment, he had finished venting and paused, so I interjected, "Bill, I don't have the benefit of having Barbara here to give her side of the story, and in all fairness to you, I really need to understand that to give you true counsel. So since she's not here, let me ask you: What would Barbara's story of your marriage sound like? Why is she interested in this Frank?"

Bill looked at me blankly. "I honestly don't know, Jim. I, um . . . I guess I've never really tried to find out. Why don't you ask her?"

The other side of the story

By this time, we were nearing the church, and Bill pointed across the parking lot. "There she is right now." Glancing in the direction he pointed, I saw a cute little red Mustang pulling into a parking spot. Bill continued to the church, and I walked toward Barbara. I reached her just as she was getting out of the car. As soon as she saw me, she bristled.

"Barbara, could I talk with you for just a few minutes?"

"Look, Jim, I know what you're going to say, and the answer is 'No.' You don't understand, and I'm not interested in another self-righteous man telling me what to do."

"Barbara, I can understand how you feel, but I'm not here to strong-arm you into being a dutiful wife. I was talking with Bill and asked him what you would say your reasons are for doing what you're doing. He said to ask you. Bill has asked me for counsel for himself, and I can't give him true advice without understanding your side of the story. All I'm asking from you is to explain your perspective."

Barbara searched my face carefully. Her dark brown eyes conveyed more hurt than anger. I could sense a warm heart beneath her prickly exterior.

"OK. But if you start pressuring me, the conversation will be over."

"It's a deal," I agreed. "Why don't we just walk down the sidewalk for a little privacy?"

We started in the same direction Bill and I had just come from, and Barbara shared with me why she found Frank so irresistible. She knew she wouldn't be happy with Frank long term, she told me, but he filled a huge void for her at present. What she shared with me confirmed what I had suspected.

Back to Bill

"Bill," I said after my conversation with Barbara, "I understand where you're coming from, but the truth of the matter is that the convenience store clerk has one thing going for him that you don't."

Disbelief spread over Bill's face. "And what could that possibly be, Jim?"

"He understands how to open your wife's heart—and you don't."

"What do you mean, 'open her heart'?"

"What I mean is that you have failed to provide emotional security for Barbara. You've done a good job providing financial security—and I'm not knocking that—but you've got to understand that a woman needs emotional security even more than she needs financial security. This other man, who seems like such a loser next to you, knows how to convey to her that he understands her, cherishes her, and connects with her.

"Now, I don't condone what Barbara is doing in any way, but the emotional connection this man offers her is such a powerful attraction to her that she is willing to risk everything for it—financial security, a good reputation, and, yes, even her eternal salvation."

Bill looked at me like I had just clobbered him with a two-by-four. "Are you telling me, Jim, that *I* am part of the problem?"

"I'm telling you that you hold the key to the problem. If you loved Barbara with principled, intentional love as Christ loves His people, she would find no attraction in Frank."

Bill couldn't believe what he was hearing. "Come on, Jim. You can't be serious!"

"Bill, I'm very serious. Most men I talk to are defensive about their role in marriage problems. They see their wives as the problems. They think that if their wife just weren't so emotional and would get her act together, things would be fine. But God knows that we men tend to be blind to our character deficiencies, and He sometimes uses our wives to get our attention about the areas He wants to address with us.

"Can you think of anything that God would want to develop in us that is more basic than learning to love our wives as Christ loves the church? Think about it. If we don't know how to cherish and care for our own brides as Christ would, do we really know how to care for the bride of Christ—His church? So many men I meet are zealous about their church offices and evangelism while their own wives are starving for a bit of tender affection. These men have a defensiveness—a huge blind spot—that keeps them from owning their real responsibility to God and their wives; and wives can't fix that just by smiling sweetly and pretending everything is OK."

Bill was listening—really listening—and he motioned for me to continue.

"If you learn to filter everything you think, say, and do through God, you can break this cycle of craziness that you and Barbara are presently on. Your lack of love for her fuels her disrespect for you, which fuels your lack of love for her—and round and round the cycle goes. You can interrupt this downward spiral by giving God complete access to you—your thoughts, your motivations, your emotions, and purposes—and then intentionally loving Barbara with nothing in it for you."

Bill got a strange look on his face. "What do you mean, 'nothing in it for me'? Didn't God create her to be my 'help meet'? Isn't she supposed to be there for me? Isn't that her God-given role?"

"You're right that God created woman to be a helper to her husband, but a lot of us men have grossly distorted what that means. We've made it mean that we are the boss—therefore our needs and wishes come first, while our wives' needs are secondary and, far too often, optional.

"Our model and pattern is Christ. Can you imagine Christ entering a town and scoping out the women? Would He evaluate them according to who had the nicest hair, the prettiest face, or the sexiest figure? Can you imagine Him stomping into Lazarus's house, flopping down on the sofa, grabbing the remote, and hollering, 'Why isn't dinner ready yet? What have you done all day, anyway?' "

"Of course not!" Bill answered. "He came to *serve*—not to exploit. But Jim, I *do* serve my wife. I go to work every day and pay the bills and mow the lawn."

"Yes, you do, and that's commendable. But it's very easy to go through the motions while our hearts aren't really in it—and then feel upset when we don't get the expected return on our investment." Bill wasn't quite convinced yet, and I continued. "For a man, following Christ means that he enters his home as a savior, and his wife's real needs are his primary concern—not second place or optional. His weary wife can come to him and find rest, strength, and understanding, because he is there to care for her—period. The interesting thing is that wives find this kind of husband irresistible!"

"Really, Jim? Is that what Barbara is looking for?" Bill was still puzzled.

"Let me say it a different way. Think of Jesus and the woman at the well. She was a messed-up woman that the world viewed as trash. But Jesus saw her through different eyes—the eyes of transforming love—and He touched her deepest need. He understood her heart. He loved her for who she was—not for what He could get out of her. And her heart opened to Him! She loved to serve Him. She couldn't do enough for Him!

"That's how God designed it to work between you and Barbara. When she senses that you understand her, that you cherish her heart, and treasure her for who she is rather than what she does for you, she will most likely blossom into a better helpmate than you could ever hope for. It will be in her heart to serve you and to respond to you."

Bill isn't unusual

Bill is not unlike most men. He has good intentions, believes he is a good husband, and is honestly baffled by Barbara's response—or I should say, lack of response—to him. The problem with Bill is a problem common to most men I talk to—they don't understand their wives.

Women have been the brunt of a lot of jokes by men who see them as mysterious, incomprehensible, and impossible to understand. They don't feel that way while they are courting their wives, but when the love potion wears off and real life sets in, a crack appears in the sidewalk of mutual sensitivity. Usually, the wife notices right away. Often, the husband does not. And the crack begins to widen until, far too often, it becomes a gaping abyss.

That's why Peter urged men to live with their wives in an understanding way. In other words, be sensitive to your wife's spirit. Don't write her off because she thinks differently than you do. When you seek to understand your wife, you will be able to meet her deepest need—which is love. By becoming "swift to hear, [and] slow to speak,"[1] you can build a bridge over the chasm.

One of the most startling breakthroughs in my marriage was when I realized that Sally is different than Jim! It was like someone turned on a light, and I said, "Aha! I see it now." When I was dating Sally, I liked the fact that she was different than me. She looked different, she smelled different, and she talked different. After we got married, I couldn't figure out what was wrong with her. Why didn't she *think* like me? When I finally grasped that God made her different than me for a reason, I could begin to treasure her rather than trying to remake her. When she felt treasured, she opened up to me like a fragrant rose.

Over the years, I've learned from Sally—and from many other women

---

1. James 1:19.

we've counseled in our ministry—five key areas that spell love to a wife. Here they are: affection, honor, transparency, understanding, and commitment.

Five keys to your wife's heart

1. Affection. It's hard for many men to grasp how intensely important affection is to a woman, but for women, it is the cement of the relationship. Without it, everything goes to pieces. Genuine, selfless affection is synonymous with security, closeness, protection, comfort, and approval. It sends important messages:

- "I'm here for you and you are my priority."
- "I'll take care of you and protect you."
- "I want to understand you."
- "I'm concerned about what concerns you, and I'm here to help you face it."
- "I'm proud of you."

It's hard to overestimate how much these strong affirmations mean to a woman. To the typical wife, you can hardly give too many of them. If your wife is like most women, the emotional security you create for her by showing her affection means more to her even than financial security.

In a survey that Jeff and Shaunti Feldhahn conducted for their book *For Men Only*, they asked women the following question: "If you had to choose, would you rather endure financial struggles, or would you rather endure struggles arising from insecurity or a lack of closeness in your relationship?" Seven out of ten married women said they would rather endure financial struggles than face emotional insecurity in their relationship.

That's hard for most of us men to come to terms with. Like Bill, most of us truly believe we are building security for our wives by working hard to provide for them financially. We feel like we live under impossible expectations—work long enough and hard enough to provide a good lifestyle, but still be home by six o'clock every night to engage with the family. Having to give our wives affection often feels like just one more thing to add to our to-do list, and we're not even sure where to start.

On top of that, most men view affection as a preliminary, leading up to the main event: sexual intimacy. In their efficient way of thinking, they figure they might as well skip the preliminaries and just get into the main event—then they wonder why their wives seem cold. But women need affection just for the sake of affection—not only as a prelude to sex.

Barbara had been deeply offended by Bill in this area. His efforts to show her affection were met with a great deal of suspicion because she sensed he was just after "one thing." I encouraged Bill to separate affection from sex in his mind and be willing to love her just for her—without looking for the payoff.

Many men haven't been trained how to do this and wonder where to start. Here are some ideas. This process may feel awkward at first because you're starting a new habit, but in time, it will become second nature—so don't give up.

- Tell her often that you love her—verbally and with little notes.
- Catch her eye across a crowded room and send her a look that says, "You're special to me! No one here is more important to me than you."
- Call her during the day to see how she is doing.
- Bring her flowers occasionally.
- Remember special events (birthdays, anniversaries, and holidays) with simple gifts and/or meaningful cards.
- Communicate your schedule and plans with her so that she knows what to expect. For example, call her from work to tell her when you will be home—and then be there.
- Share conversation with her. Ask her about her day and then look into her eyes and listen to what she says. Tell her about your day too.
- Be open to talk about anything.
- Include her in your recreational plans.
- Let her know you like her company and want her with you.
- Enter into activities she enjoys—even if you don't.
- Help her with tasks such as washing the dishes after dinner or bathing the kids.
- Touch her in tender, nonsexual ways—hold her hand, hug her, touch her gently when near her, kiss her before you go to work and when you come home.

If you are like most men who have put expressions of affection to your wife on the back burner, I recommend taking your wife for a walk and explaining to her that you love her very deeply but that you haven't understood how to express it appropriately. Tell her that you want to learn and that anything she shares with you to help you learn will be welcomed by you. Let her know that you will not be looking for a payoff. You want to love her for her—with nothing in it for you. If you're courageous enough, ask her to rate the items on the above list according to what touches her heart the most. And by all means, ask God to prompt you by His Holy

Spirit when an opportunity arises to demonstrate affection to your wife.

2. Honor. If affection is the cement of the relationship, then honor is one of the bricks. You honor your wife when you cherish her above all others—and that includes your visual choices. This is where many men have a difficult spiritual challenge to meet. They've bought the devil's food cake, which comes straight from hell. The devil presents an image before your mind of something that's not yours and whispers, oh, so persuasively, "This is just what you need. It will satisfy your desires." But when you bite into it, you find it doesn't deliver what you expected—and so he entices you to take another bite, and yet another, of his deadly cake. You're always hoping to find satisfaction but never realizing it.

We live in a sex-saturated society, and everywhere we go, we are confronted with images of physically attractive women dressed (or rather, undressed) in suggestive attire—both in real life and in the media. Because of the way men are wired, we are naturally drawn to those images, and the devil offers us his deadly cake: "This is real beauty. This is a real woman. You would be happier if you could have her. Let your mind fondle her just for a little while." When you allow those kinds of thoughts to marinate in your brain—and you go home, and your wife has had a hard day and doesn't look the best or smell the freshest or talk the sweetest—guess what? Your brain goes, "Yuck!"

Then when nighttime comes, and you want to make love, your lovemaking is all about satisfying yourself rather than connecting with your wife. A woman can sense that very quickly, and it hits her at her very core—especially if she already has doubts about her adequacy as a woman. Wives have a deep longing to know that they are not in competition—that they are cherished for who they are in God's eyes more than how they compare with the latest *Cosmopolitan* model.

As I shared these thoughts with Bill, he got a bit agitated. "But Jim, Barbara used to be attractive. Her figure was slim and trim when I married her. Now she's just plain pudgy and wrinkled. To be perfectly honest, I don't like to look at her."

"Bill, let me tell you how I see your wife. I don't see her as fat or thin, dressed or undressed. I see her heart. She has a tender heart that longs to be loved and treasured. I noticed something this morning while I was preaching. Do you remember those two babies who started crying?"

"Yeah, that woman has twins and can't control one—much less both of them."

"Well, you probably didn't see it from where you were sitting, but someone moved over to help that mother quiet her children. Do you know who it was?"

"It was probably Barbara. She loves little children and has a way with them and loves to help other mothers when they're overloaded."

"You're right. It was Barbara. I didn't know then about the problems you and she are having, but I remember thinking, *That woman has a servant's heart*. I found something to treasure about Barbara before I even met her. Surely as her husband you can find more than that."

Many men find this a tough assignment because their minds have been programmed to go the other direction for so long. But the mind can be changed. The key is to enter into the fight of faith in order to bring all the thoughts into captivity to Christ—including the ones about comparing their wives to other women. We must close as many avenues of temptation as possible and then, with God's help, design a fire escape so that we know what to do when those images come parading across the mind.

For me, that is one big plus for country living. I can walk out of my house at any time and look in any direction, and there is nothing that my eyes can't safely rest on. I don't have TV, and I burn all the unsolicited junk that comes in the mail. That closes a lot of avenues for the devil's food cake. But I do have to go into town, and Sally and I travel a lot. I can't always avoid the billboards, the magazines at the gas stations and grocery stores, or the plunging necklines of the twenty-year-old cashiers. That's when my fire escape serves me well. God helped me plan it many years ago, so that what was once a discipline is now second nature for me.

When those images come, instead of letting them trigger impure thoughts, I think of Sally. I think of all the things I love about her and what a treasure she is to me. Sure, she's nearly sixty years old, and some things about her aren't as firm and smooth as they used to be, but I don't even notice that. She is gorgeous to me—even when she has rollers in her hair! Her heart is pure gold. The more I think about her and what I love about her, the more eager I am to see her. And when I do see her, I'm excited—even if she's had a hard day. She knows that she doesn't have to compete with anyone or anything for me. I honor her with my thoughts and with my eyes. And when I unite with her in intimacy, it's angel's food cake because she has my heart, and I have hers.

3. *Transparency.* When Bill was courting Barbara, he was totally open with her. He shared his dreams, his yearnings, his fears, and his failures. He spoke heart-to-heart with Barbara. Their openness with each other was something they could literally feel. But once they got married and the stress of their differences hit them, Bill quit doing that. Barbara would attempt to get close to him by saying, "You've been kind of quiet lately. What's on your mind?"

"Nothing," Bill would reply.

Now, Bill is not unusual. Almost every husband I've counseled with has done that. I did it too. When I was courting Sally, I loved to talk with her about my plans, my dreams, and my life. After we got married, the news and sports seemed a lot more intriguing.

As I've thought about it, I think I understand why. During courtship, a man is seeking to discover the woman of his dreams. He's met this lovely creature, and he's wondering if she is the one. How will she respond to him? Will she understand him, admire him, and enter into his dreams and plans? Will he be able to win her heart? It is an exhilarating adventure.

But once he concludes that his dream has come true, he's satisfied. He no longer feels the need to share and be open. He doesn't understand that his openness communicated love to her in a big way and that she thrives on his transparent talk.

If a husband doesn't keep up honest, open communication with his wife, he undermines her trust. To feel secure, a wife must be able to trust her husband to give her accurate information about his past, present, and the future. What has he done? What is he thinking or doing right now? What plans does he have? If she can't trust the signals he sends (or if he refuses to send any signals), she has no foundation on which to build a solid relationship. Instead of adjusting to him, she always feels off balance; instead of growing up with him, she grows away from him.

A wise husband is honest with his wife about what's happening inside his mind and heart. While the movies may glorify the strong, silent man, it is the man who is transparent with his wife that will enjoy her admiration. Transparency opens her heart and draws her into his inner circle. You might be tempted to think that she won't respect you if she knows about some of your struggles, but the reality is just the opposite. When you are real with her, her heart will be drawn to you.

When I explained this to Bill, he gave me a blank look. "Where do I start, Jim? I feel like I'm light-years away from Barbara. How do I close the gap?"

"Well, a good place to start would be where I started with Sally when we moved to the wilderness. I set aside a regular time each day to talk with her. It doesn't matter if you feel like it or not, turn off the TV, put down the newspaper, get off the Internet or whatever else consumes your free time, and make yourself available to her. Take her for a walk down the street or a drive in the car or sit on the porch together and begin to open up to her. God will help you learn how to be transparent again.

"When I started doing that with Sally, it seemed awkward to me at first, but as I began to share again with her my dreams, fears, plans, failures, joys, and aspirations, she became my best friend once more. She thrived on my openness. She said it made her feel 'one' with me. Instead of becoming more and more independent from each other, we began to grow closer. Believe me, it is worth the investment of your effort and time!"

4. *Understanding.* Shortly after we moved to the mountains, my Sally was having a really down day. By early evening, she couldn't take it anymore. Slipping quietly out of the house, she disappeared into the woods. I didn't even notice she was gone until I needed to ask her a question.

"Boys, do you know where Mother is?" I asked Matthew and Andrew as they sanded away on one of their latest woodworking projects.

"Umm," Andrew looked up. "I saw her heading off in the direction of her favorite stump a little while ago—you know, the one she goes to when she's really upset. She didn't look too happy. Maybe you should wait till she calms down a bit."

Now I had *two* reasons to find Sally, so I headed off in the direction of that good, old stump and, sure enough, there she was, perched on it with her face buried in her hands. The moment she looked at me, I could see distress written all over her.

"What's the matter, honey?" I asked.

You might have thought I had turned on a water faucet. Tears streamed down her cheeks as she began to spill out her struggles. I listened very carefully, and I identified what I believed was the problem.

When she had finished her tale of woe about giving way to appetite again and explained how out of control she felt, I was ready with some very helpful advice—and I didn't hesitate to give it to her! In spite of my sincere intention to relieve her distress, I accomplished just the opposite. Instead of drying her tears and thanking me for being her knight in shining armor, Sally's tears flowed all the faster, and her words came in short little gulps. "I . . . ," *sniff, sniff,* "don't need you . . . ," *sniff,* "to tell me . . . ," *sniff, sniff,* "what to do," *sniff, sniff.* "I already know . . . all that."

"What do you mean you don't need me to tell you what to do?" I wondered out loud. "Then, why did you tell me your problem?" I was mystified. Hadn't I solved her problem? Why hadn't it relieved her distress?

"I don't need advice, Jim," *sniff, sniff.* "I just want some compassion—to know you haven't given up on me. That's all."

That made no sense to me. I couldn't relate to what she was saying. So without another word, I left and joined the boys in the garage to finish a project I had been working on. But I couldn't get Sally's words out of my mind—*"I just want some compassion."*

Finally, I said out loud, "God, are You trying to show me something? What is it that You want me to do with Sally?"

Startled, my boys looked up at me—then shrugged their shoulders and went back to work.

And that still, small Voice whispered, *"Just give her a hug and tell her you love her."*

"That's all?" It didn't make sense to my efficient, problem-solving mind.

"Yes, Jim. It will mean the world to her. Just try it."

I wrestled with that thought for another five minutes and then headed back to the woods. Sally was still huddled forlornly on that stump and didn't look up when I reached her. Tenderly, I lifted her chin to look into her tear-stained face. "How about a hug?" I offered.

She burst into tears again, but this time they were tears of relief. She stood up, and I wrapped my arms around her and whispered as gently as I could, "I love you, Sally. I'll be with you through this thing. I believe you'll work it out, and I'll be by your side." She just melted into my arms and stayed there for a long while. When at last she stepped back, there was a little sparkle starting to rekindle in her lovely dark eyes. "Thank you, Jim. That's just what I needed."

As we walked back to the house together, I was shaking my head. Sally didn't want to be "fixed." She just wanted to be understood and affirmed. Figuring this out was a big breakthrough for me.

My natural approach was to filter out her emotions and focus on solving the problem. But I'm learning that sometimes I need to let the "problem" fade into the background and simply identify with her emotions. She wants my support more than my solutions. Often, she already knows what she needs to do. She just wants to know that I understand her, that I believe in her, and that I will go through it with her. Now I try to understand her emotions and help her work through them rather than just shutting them down.

Sometimes I'm not sure what Sally really needs, and so I'll ask, "Honey, shall we try to solve this thing or do you just need to know that I'm in it with you?" More often than not, she wants simply to be heard and affirmed.

5. *Commitment.* As a teenager, I dated a lot of girls, and there was something I liked about each one. When I met Sally, I was dating three or four girls at a time. Judy was my Monday and Thursday girl; Betty filled the slot on Tuesdays and Fridays; and Sunday was for Tina. Sally was my Saturday and Wednesday girl. As time went on, I found myself looking forward to Saturdays and Wednesdays more and more. There was just no one like Sally. We clicked. We shared the same values and interests. Our likes and dislikes were compatible. Our temperaments blended. We loved to work and play together. We both willingly adapted to each other. And last, but not least,

there was electricity between us—I mean, we had a real spark!

I soon lost interest in Tina, and Sally took her place on Sunday. When I was with Judy, all I could think of was spending time with Sally. So Sally took over Mondays and Thursdays. Betty caught the drift of things, and soon Sally became my all-time girl, and I pledged myself to her and only her. In other words, I made a commitment. In that commitment, she knew that I was there for her—always. That commitment deepened and broadened. I vowed to keep myself only for her for the rest of my life, and in due time, we stood at the altar together.

My commitment after marriage meant more than sharing physical intimacy exclusively with Sally. It also meant that I would engage my energies to serve her best interests. My commitment would be spelled out in the nuts and bolts of everyday living. For example, I shouldered the responsibility and privilege of providing adequate financial support for Sally—even if that meant shoveling manure for a living. Fortunately, I didn't have to do that, but I was—and am—willing to do whatever needs to be done to provide adequately for Sally.

I plan my daily schedule to meet not only my needs but hers as well. Sally can depend on me to carry out my share of the home duties and responsibilities and to sacrifice my interests in order to pick up more than my share of the home duties when needed. I also consider both her needs and mine as I strive to balance work and play, socializing and solitude.

When I first got married, I didn't understand my role as the spiritual leader of the family, but in time God awakened me to that calling. I am now deeply committed to understanding and ministering to the spiritual needs of my family.

Underlying all these expressions of commitment is the effort to enter into and maintain a "best friend" relationship with Sally. She knows that my heart is hers and that I am committed to making our home and marriage the best that it can possibly be under God.

These five areas—expressing affection, honor, transparency, understanding, and commitment—have become a way of life for me. Not that I'm perfect in them, but I am consistent in them. And this consistency has provided the stability that Sally has always longed for in her heart of hearts.

Bill listened to what I had to say and eventually restored that which was missing with Barbara. Oh, she didn't respond at first. Thirty days went by. Sixty days. Then ninety days—and Barbara was still not convinced. Bill hung in there. He had caught the vision of loving Barbara with nothing in it for him—and he wasn't giving up. After what seemed a very long time, Barbara began to respond, and Frank held no appeal for her anymore. She not only had her Bill back, but now she found him irresistible again and became "focused on him." And that's the title of the next chapter.

Study Questions for Chapter 4

1. On a scale of one to ten, how would your wife rate your marriage both on the good days and the not-so-good days? If you don't know—ask her.
2. Do you know how to open your wife's heart?
3. Would your wife say you are "focused on her"?
4. Does your wife receive the affection necessary to see you as irresistible?
5. Does your definition of "help meet" lead you to view your wife's needs as secondary while yours are primary?
6. What will you do today to express affection to your wife?
7. Do you honor your wife—even in your thought life?
8. Does your wife find you transparent? If not, will you begin today to cultivate transparency with her?
9. Will you seek to live with your wife in an understanding way?
10. In what ways is God asking you to make a deeper commitment to your wife?

CHAPTER 5

Focused on Him

Who can find a virtuous wife?
For her worth is far above rubies.
The heart of her husband safely trusts her;
So he will have no lack of gain.
She does him good and not evil
All the days of her life.

—*Proverbs 31:10–12*

[Note: This chapter is written especially for wives, but husbands are welcome to read along!]

The other day, Sally asked me a question that really got me to thinking. We were having our usual swing time—just reminiscing together about our lives.

For those of you who don't know us or who haven't been to our annual "open house," Sally and I live in a quaint log cabin eight miles south of the Canadian border right across the north fork of the Flathead River from Glacier National Park. Out in front of our cabin—and just to the side—hangs a double swing suspended between two stately Douglas firs. Our son, Andrew, built the original swing almost fifteen years ago, and Sally and I have developed a routine of sitting in that swing every day at noon and reconnecting with each other for half an hour.

This particular day was spectacular! Fresh snow capped the magnificent peaks that stretch themselves in front of us. The larches were turning gold, and the sky was a crystal clear blue. The air was crisp, but the sun was warm—as warm as our hearts were for each other.

Sally asked, "So, Jim, what was it that attracted you to me over all those other girls you dated back in our high school years?"

I had dated a lot of different girls—from the popular cheerleaders to the quiet girls. It seemed like I always had girlfriends. I don't know why, because I was a very shy, quiet, reserved young man. But that's the way it was. I enjoyed being with these girls—most of the time—but I never really fell for any of them. Until I met Sally.

There was something different about Sally. She filled a void—a need in me—that that drew me to her like a paper clip to a magnet. I didn't understand it at the time, nor could I have labeled it then, but I understand it now. I can summarize what she did for me then and what she still does today into five areas. We have found that I'm not the only husband who responds to efforts made in these five areas. They represent the basic needs of nearly all the husbands we have met. So, wives, here are some things you can tune into to become irresistible again to your husband.

Five keys to your husband's heart

1. Admiration and respect. I remember walking from chemistry class to PE when I was eighteen years old. I had started looking forward to that part of the day, because there was something about it that made me feel really good. It had something to do with the fact that Sally sat right behind me in chemistry class, and afterward, every day she walked with me to my PE class.

I'll never forget what I felt as she looked up at me with those lovely eyes as we walked down the hallway! It's sort of how my grandkids look at me now when I push a tree over with my tractor or split some firewood with my ax. They stand in awe with wide eyes. *Grandpa can do anything!*

Well, that's how Sally made me feel. She just knew I was the best! I was physically fit, had golden hair and green eyes, and I was her champion. I can't tell you how it feels to have someone look at you with such admiring eyes. It builds tremendous emotional security, affirmation, and connection. I was too shy to discuss it with anyone, but, oh, how I thrived on it! I never tired of it and longed for more.

You might find it hard to believe now, but I was very insecure in those early years. I had few talents and skills and, quite frankly, I felt stupid when compared with my peers. I saw myself as incompetent and felt embarrassed much of the time. I viewed my peers as smart, suave, and skilled. Me? I was just a quiet, untalented, unintelligent kid who didn't know who he was or where he was going.

You see, I was raised in a family that expressed almost no affection, affirmation, or admiration—even for a job well done. I still remember winning the mile race at the track meet. I'd never run the mile race before and had no idea how to go about it. I figured that the idea was to just run as fast as I could and not let anyone pass me—and that's what I did! They almost had to do CPR on me by the time I got to the finish line! But my sheer tenacity—and perhaps, individual pride—won the race that day.

I felt kind of good about winning. I wasn't used to that. But when I got home and told my family about it, they just kind of smiled and changed the subject. I figured it was nothing—and that *I* was nothing.

So, when I walked down that hallway with Sally every day and she looked at me with those eyes that said, "You are something! I believe in you!" I soaked it up like a thirsty sponge. Her believing in me helped me to believe in myself and gave me the confidence to become the man I am today.

She's still doing the same thing! She makes sure I know that I'm on the top of her list as a man, that there's no other guy in the world that competes with me for her admiration. No, it doesn't happen that way 100 percent of the time. We have our little tiffs from time to time, but they are short lived.

Sally lets me know that I'm a good provider and that she has confidence in me. She says, "Jim, you can do anything!" and she really believes it too. She loves my mischievous side and thanks me for how I oversee our house, profession, and social life. In fact, she's developed a phrase that she uses in both public and private: "That's my man!" You should hear how she says it! Sometimes she says it after I step out of the pulpit. Sometimes she says it when I've done the yard work or helped her with chores inside the home. That one-liner tells me, "There's no one quite like you! I married the right man! You've become everything to me!"

Oh, that every husband could know and experience this! As I've talked to husbands around the globe, I've found that they all—almost without exception—crave this kind of admiration and respect. Wives, look for ways to give this admiration and respect to your husbands. Ask the Holy Spirit to whisper in your ear each time you can honestly affirm your husband and remind you to tell him in your own way, "That's my man!" Then do it again and again until it becomes habit.

Maybe you're thinking that your husband doesn't deserve this kind of treatment. You might be right. He may not deserve it. But he *needs* it—just as much as you need unconditional love. How would you feel if your husband told you that he respects you but can't love you? Most women would feel devastated. Men are equally devastated when their wives communicate by their words or their actions: "I love you, but I can't respect you." To a man, this feels like contempt for who he is as a person. Your husband needs to feel that you believe in him—in the real man deep inside that is perhaps hidden by pride or fear or a poor history.

Ask God to help you to see your husband through His eyes, to place the same value on him that God does, and to show it in tangible ways. Many wives are simply not aware of this deep need in their husbands and so, even though they value things about their husbands, they don't think to tell them. So, start by telling your husband what you admire and respect about him. If you have a hard time thinking of something to admire about your husband, pray about it and ask God to help you get started. Keep a journal of all the things you appreciate about him—his talents, his work, his looks, his help around the home, even skills that he hasn't developed yet. Affirm him in every way you honestly can.

In areas that you can't affirm, express your disagreement respectfully. There are times when it is appropriate to give your husband honest feedback about how he affects you and what you need from him. But how you handle this makes a tremendous difference. Yelling at him, "You are so sloppy! Can't you ever pick up after yourself?" carries a lot of unspoken disrespect. Approaching him with an even tone of voice and an understanding smile and saying, "I know you've got a lot on your plate right now, sweetheart, but it would really help me if you could drop your clothes in the laundry basket instead of the middle of the bathroom," conveys respect—and is far more likely to get results! It sounds simple, but it can make a big difference between a tension-filled marriage and a well-oiled marriage.

Avoid "mothering" your husband. Gina and Fred are good friends of mine and love each other deeply. But Gina has a habit that really rubs Fred the wrong way. "Fred, sit over here." "Wipe your nose, Fred." "Take off your shoes before you come into the house." "Don't forget to thank the pastor for his sermon yesterday." "Remember to take your vitamins." Fred is a successful physician who manages his practice with a great deal of competence—without his wife overseeing everything he does.

At first glance, Gina's "helpful" reminders and instructions seem like plain bossiness, but they convey a deeper message to Fred—disrespect. He feels like a little boy with a mother, more than a knight in shining armor with his beautiful maiden. No man likes to feel that way.

Instead, treat your husband like a VIP! Instead of belittling him, make sure your words and actions affirm him.

2. Companionship. I'll never forget my first date with Sally. I put her on the back of my motorcycle and headed out to High Cliff State Park. I had tried doing that with a lot of the other girls I dated, and they had balked at the idea—but not Sally. She hopped right on behind me. As you can imagine, that put her in a somewhat "intimate" position with me for our first date, and she didn't know what to do with her hands. She tried several different positions that didn't work and finally rested them lightly on my hips, doing her best not to make too much body contact.

When we arrived at the park, I headed for the limestone cliffs. I don't know what there was about those cliffs, but I loved to climb them. They fascinated me! I wondered if Sally would be scared and sit at the bottom of the cliffs like most girls I'd known. Not her! She was right there with me. No, she'd never climbed before, but she was game to try!

I liked that! I asked her out again—and again! It seemed that no matter what I did, she would be my shadow. We went hiking, swam in the quarry, cruised the streets on my motorcycle, played football and racquetball, and even went hunting together.

I can still see her all dressed up in her camo outfit. She marched up to me, put her hands on her hips, and asked me in her toughest voice, "So where do you want me to stake out?" When she stood to shoot the 12-gauge shotgun, the kick was so powerful that it threw her off her feet, but she didn't complain. She was game for more!

I was hooked! Sally became my best friend—even more than my male buddies. No, she wasn't as good or gifted as me in a lot of these areas, and I didn't expect her to match me. But her heart was with me. She was always by my side, doing her best. She may not have loved all these activities, but she loved being with me!

I didn't know then that I *needed* a companion, but God did. In fact, He planned it that way. Even Adam, in his perfect state, was lonely. God gave Eve to Adam, and He gave Sally to me. She became inseparably linked to my life and joys—and she still is today!

She goes skydiving and scuba diving with me, backpacking and canoeing into the wilderness. Recently, some friends invited us to go hang gliding with them—and Sally will be in on it too! She's sixty years old, but she's still by my side, still entering into my adventures and activities.

She's my companion in everyday life too. Whether it's washing the car, cutting firewood, or ministering on the road, Sally is involved. When I return from a trip, she meets me at the door, interested to know how things went for me. Oh, that means so much to me!

I have a friend whose passion is racquetball. His wife doesn't play, but he wants her there for every game. He wants her to watch him, to console him when he has an off day, and to cheer for him when he nabs those killer shots. Even though she can't match his racquetball skills, he thrives on her companionship. It opens his heart and endears her to him.

Another friend loves old cars. I mean, I've never seen anyone get so excited about old chrome bumpers and mahogany instrument panels. His favorite entertainment is to go to old car shows—and his wife always accompanies him. No, she's not into old cars. In fact, she wishes he'd get rid of a few of the ones in their shop. But she's into *him,* and she gets into it *for* him! She goes, because he's at the top of the list for her. He tells me he just loves having someone to share his thoughts with about these old cars—someone to reminisce with. Their marriage, by the way, has graduated from near divorce to irresistible!

A common stereotype paints husbands as wanting to "get away with the guys." But reality is that most married men *don't* want to abandon their wife to do guy things—at least not all the time. They want to do "guy things" with their wife. They want her to be their playmate. In fact, according to Willard Harley, spending recreational time with one's wife is second in importance only to physical intimacy for the typical husband.[1] A woman who is having fun with her husband is incredibly attractive to him.

Of course, the wife's attitude makes a big difference. Complaining, fussing, and whining break down the companionship. Be alive to your husband. Tell him that you like him and want to be with him—and then show it.

Be his companion in everyday life too. Now, that may mean something different to him than it does to you. Most wives have a deep need to talk when they are together with their husbands, and there is a place for that. But many husbands want their wives to be with them with little or no talk at all. Your very presence is energizing to them—whether it's watching a video, going for a hike, or doing a chore. They want you to be with them. This can seem pointless and baffling to women, but try it and see what it does for your husband.

A woman friend of mine described this to me. Her husband would be doing some fix-it task around the house. It was a "one-man" job, but he still wanted her to be there with him. She would try to talk to him, but he was so focused on his task that he didn't engage in conversation with her. So she would busy herself with something else. Then he would stop and ask her to be there beside him.

"Well, what do you want me to do?" she would ask.

"Nothing," he would reply. "Just be here, in case I need you."

He just wanted her presence with him. Until she understood his need for companionship, she thought he was being childish and wasting her time for no good purpose. Now she understands that being with him serves a very important purpose. It says to him in a big way, "I'm here for you! You're number one in my book! I'm your companion."

Wives, be your husband's best companion. All husbands may not be as involved in adventurous activities as I am—or they may not play racquetball or get goggle-eyed over old car shows—but study who your man is. What are his interests? What gets him excited and holds his attention? Then enter into those things with him.

3. Attractive to me. I was one of the first ones to take my seat that first day in high school chemistry class. I sat there surveying the array of beakers, bottles, and periodic tables placed strategically around the room. Out of the corner of my eye, I was vaguely aware of my classmates coming through the door and taking their seats.

---

1. Harley, 52.

Then Sally walked in. She had her books in her arm and carried herself in a certain manner. Her hair was cut in a bob, and she was wearing a rust-colored sweater that fit her form just right. It was obvious that she took a tasteful pride in her appearance. She possessed a purity, a wholesomeness, that attracted me to her—not just physically. Everything about her blended in a tasteful way that was easy on my eyes; like a beautiful flower, she was lovely to behold.

Today, she's sixty years old, but when she walks into the room, she still catches my eye. She still weighs the same as she did back in high school. She keeps up her figure, her hair, and her appearance—even when it's just the two of us around the house. Her physical appearance, combined with the sweetness of her voice and the depth of her personality, all make her very attractive to me.

Wives, take a look at your wedding picture. Now, look in the mirror. Are you who he married? Sure, we all age. Childbearing, stress, time, and hormonal changes all take their toll. But are you doing the best with what you have?

I know this hits a hot button for many women, because we live in a culture that is saturated with a false portrait of women. The media blitzes us with images of size two figures of perfect proportions—and women get the message loud and clear that their value is somehow tied to their size and shape. Many women have been driven to eating disorders and emotional distress over the unreasonable demand to become something God never designed them to be.

On the other hand, some women quit trying. They believe that " 'man looks at the outward appearance, but the Lord looks at the heart,' "[2] and so the outward appearance shouldn't matter. They feel that their husbands should treasure their hearts and not care how they look or how they present themselves.

But Proverbs 31 paints a different picture—the picture of a complete package. A virtuous woman takes care of herself—emotionally, spiritually, *and physically*.

> She girds herself with strength,
>   And strengthens her arms. . . .
> She makes tapestry for herself;
>   Her clothing is fine linen and purple.[3]

---

2. 1 Samuel 16:7.
3. Proverbs 31:17, 22.

In other words, she works with what she has, within reasonable bounds, to be the very best she can be.

Most women don't realize how much affirmation their husbands feel when their wives put forth the effort to present their best to their husbands. How would you feel if you married your husband while he was earning a good living in a successful job, and then once he hooked you, he quit his job and applied for welfare? Would you feel that you hadn't quite gotten the package you were expecting?

Imagine then, how husbands feel after they marry the woman of their dreams only to find her ballooning out of proportion and pleading that he should just love her, anyway.

Shaunti Feldhahn's book, *For Women Only,* is based on hundreds of personal and written interviews with men, including a professionally conducted survey. One of the questions she asked was, " 'Imagine your wife/significant other is overweight, wears baggy sweats when you are home, and only does her hair and makeup to go out. She hates being overweight, but nothing much changes and lately you've seen her eating more sweets. What goes through your mind?'

"Seven out of ten men indicated that they would be emotionally bothered if the woman in their life let herself go and didn't seem to want to make the effort to do something about it. Only 12 percent said it didn't bother them—and even fewer happily married, younger, churchgoing men weren't bothered."[4]

Wives, please don't misunderstand! I'm not saying you have to look like a twenty-year-old model or win the Mrs. America contest. That very thought is paralyzing to most women. But your effort to be attractive in your appearance, your personality, and your approach to your husband will draw him to you. It says to him that he is valuable to you. That he is worth sacrificing for.

Shaunti asked another question that clarifies the first: "Is this statement true or false? 'I want my wife/significant other to look good and feel energetic. It is not as important that she look just like she did the day we met. It is more important that she make the effort to take care of herself for me now.' "[5]

Here's the good news: five out of six men agreed—with regular churchgoers agreeing even more strongly. It's the *effort* you put forth for him that opens your husband's heart to you. It isn't that the results don't matter—they do. But they will be a natural by-product of your effort to take care of

---

4. Shaunti Feldhahn, *For Women Only* (Colorado Springs, Colo.: Multnomah Publishers, 2004), 161.

5. Ibid., 162.

yourself. It's your effort that means the most.

What does that mean? It might mean exchanging your baggy sweats around the house for a neat, tasteful outfit. It might mean taking a shower and doing your hair before he comes home. It might mean getting serious about a weight-loss program or revamping your wardrobe. Remember principle one: God will guide you to know what you need to do. Consult with Him and let Him empower you to be all He made you to be!

4. *Affectionate and warm.* The guys I grew up with made it a goal to get a kiss on the first date. I remember standing around with the other ninth-grade boys and listening to them brag about how they had kissed so-and-so. To them, this was big-time stuff!

I didn't get into that. Sally and I dated for months before I was brave enough to steal my first kiss. Why do I say, "steal"?

I lost my motorcycle license, because I was caught driving too fast and swerving in and out of traffic. I pulled into the Standard Oil station where I worked, and the red lights came on behind me. The police didn't just give me a ticket—they took away my license for ninety days!

So, when Sally and I would go on our dates, she would pick me up in her 1960 canary-yellow Ford. One night, as she was dropping me off, she parked in my parents' driveway. We sat in the front bench seat of the car and talked for an hour—just enjoying each other's company. I had been thinking about kissing her and finally got up my courage. With my right hand on the door handle, ensuring an immediate exit, I leaned over and gave her a quick peck on the cheek. Then I bolted out of the car as fast as I could and made a beeline for the back door!

Sally was mad! She doesn't get mad easily, but when she does—look out! She went home thoroughly steamed and marched in to her mother. "Sally, you seem upset!" her mother noted.

"That Jim!" Sally exploded. "He kissed me!"

"Well, Sally. Most girls would like that."

"Not me! I want only the man I'm going to marry to kiss me."

It took a while for her to get over it, but she finally did. I began to wonder if Sally was a "cold fish." Not that I knew much about that—but I had heard enough to know that I sure hoped she wasn't.

As our relationship grew, heart-to-heart and mind-to-mind, I found that Sally was very warm. There was something different in holding hands with Sally. Her hugs and cuddles weren't "plastic," but enduring. We connected with both spark and tingle. It wasn't just testosterone, although there was plenty of that circulating. Sally had a warmth and affection I had never experienced or known before. It was pure, deep, and meaningful.

Now, we're sixty years old. The other evening on our walk, Sally stopped me, looked up with those admiring eyes, and kissed me in such a sweet and connected way. It warmed my heart, and later I left a note on her desk that said, "Sally, your kisses were particularly sweet on our walk tonight!" A little later, I found the same note back on my desk with her reply, "So, too, were yours! ☺"

Wives, I can't express to you enough the value in true, daily affection. Men especially are "empty cups" here. I'm not just talking about when you climb into bed. I'm talking about conveying your heart to his.

Romance does not need to end at marriage. It needs to be pursued and perfected daily. It needs to be nurtured as a way of life!

The guys my dad worked with always went to the bars and girlie shows after work before they went home. My dad never did, and I used to wonder why. Now, I know. He knew what was waiting at home—a warm, loving, affectionate wife. He knew he would find her freshly showered and perfumed, hair brushed, house cleaned, table set, and a hot meal ready. She would greet him with tenderness and affection and then proceed to sit with him on the front porch and connect.

Physical intimacy and touch is vitally important to your husband. If that is an area of difficulty for you, don't shrug it off. Although it may not be especially important for you in the relationship, it is very important for most husbands—not because he is fleshly (although that is an important issue to identify and address), but because that's how God wired him. A husband needs physical intimacy in the same way you need emotional intimacy. Many couples reach a standoff, because the wife finds it difficult to engage physically without a genuine emotional connection and the husband finds it equally difficult to engage emotionally without physical intimacy.

Recently, I talked with a couple who have a good marriage in many ways but who have found themselves caught in this vicious cycle. He was overly busy with work and home projects and had slipped into a rather focused mode of getting things done. He didn't have time to hear about her day and process her emotions with her, and she felt distant from him. When he approached her physically, she felt used. Her heart just wasn't in it, so she withdrew from him. He felt hurt by her apparent lack of interest in him and withdrew further into his projects—which had the effect on her of more emotional isolation.

It was a self-defeating cycle that went round and round—faster and faster. By the time they talked to me, both were confused and concerned about where this was all heading and what to do about it.

I encouraged them, "You have to carry out principle two daily—to meet the other person's needs—and in time your feelings and emotions will follow. Bob, you need to consciously choose to affirm Brenda. Compliment her. Leave little love notes for her to find. Make eye contact with her that says, 'You're special to me.' And Brenda, you don't have to wait until your emotional cup is full before you make love with Bob. As you respond to the promptings of the Holy Spirit encouraging you to give those little attentions to Bob, and as you see Bob engaging more often with you, your emotions and feelings will return. Entered into daily, principles one and two will restore the balance of love between you."

About two months later, we talked again. Their marriage was becoming revitalized. Bob was developing a sensitivity to Brenda's emotional needs, and Brenda was opening up like a spring flower to Bob's physical needs. They were truly experiencing being irresistible again!

Unfortunately, not all couples find it that easy to solve these problems. Another husband confided in me that every time he puts his arm around his wife in bed, she comes unglued—and he doesn't know why. When I talked with his wife, I discovered that her father used to molest her as a teenager. So now, every time her husband moves toward her in a physical way, the memories of her physical trauma, together with the unresolved emotional pain of the past, rise up to overwhelm her.

"Have you told your husband about this?" I asked.

"No, I couldn't do that," she replied, as the tears streamed down her face.

I don't blame this woman for her wounds and her inability to respond to her husband. She is one of the walking wounded—devastated by a hit-and-run driver early in life. What happened to her is not her fault. And still, the responsibility for dealing with her disability lies in her court. She must find help to deal with her past if her marriage is ever to move out of the "stalled" position.

If that's you, don't take on guilt. But do take the initiative for getting better. Ask God for help. Seek a Christian counselor trained in the area of sexual abuse. Find friends who will support you as you work through your hurt. Let your husband know what you're dealing with, so that he knows you're not just rejecting him.

Proper physical responsiveness to your husband communicates to him that you're his girl. Your physical response to his touch opens his emotional well-being. It tells him that he has all of you and that you accept all of him. When this is lacking, he feels jilted, deprived, and put off. When physical intimacy happens, he senses a fulfillment and a depth of oneness with you.

You may have to work at this, fine-tune it, communicate about it, but for the sake of an irresistible marriage, you need to make it a priority.

5. *My helper.* "The LORD God said, 'It is not good for the man to be alone. I will make a helper suitable for him.' "[6]

Sally was my helper even before we were engaged. I worked at the Standard Oil gas station during the years when attendants pumped your gas, washed your windows, and checked your oil and tires—all for twenty-five cents a gallon!

One evening, I was standing in the office visiting with Betty. At that point in my life, I dated different girls on different nights of the week—but I didn't tell them that! Betty was my "Friday girl," and she had come over to visit me in her shiny, blue Camaro. She was kind of eyeing me and coaxing, "When are you going to take me out again, Jim?"

I was just starting to reply when I caught sight of something that put me in gear in a hurry—a canary-yellow Ford pulling up to the intersection across from the station! *That's Sally!* I thought. *Oh boy, I've got to get Betty out of here fast!*

"Listen, Betty, I've got work to do. Let me see you off."

Hurriedly, I ushered Betty out to her car and helped her in. I hoped she didn't notice the panic on my face as I blurted, "I'll see you Friday night at the dance."

Sally pulled in right next to Betty and put her car in park just as Betty shifted to reverse and backed out. My head was spinning. I looked over to Sally. She got out of her old Ford dressed in a cute pair of shorts with a big smile on her face. I felt as guilty as sin itself. I walked around to meet her in kind of a daze. She opened the back door of her car and pulled out a wooden tray covered with a big napkin. When she lifted the napkin, my mouth started watering! That tray was loaded with fresh buttered corn, hot biscuits, hash brown potatoes, a gorgeous cheeseburger with all the trimmings, and a big, frosty root beer float. Boy, was I impressed!

The difference between Betty and Sally wasn't lost on me. Betty had a new Camaro and knew that I got hungry on my evening shift. But when she came to see me, the only thing on her mind was what I could do for her. Sally drove an old Ford, but her chief reason for visiting me was to do something for me. Betty was mostly interested in herself, while Sally was interested in what she could do for me. What a contrast! It wasn't long before Sally was the only girl I cared to date.

As time went on, I discovered that this wasn't an unusual thing for Sally to do. Sally has a true servant's heart, and she couldn't serve me enough. She

---

6. Genesis 2:18, NIV.

wasn't doing it to get her man on the hook. This was the way she loved me. No other girl did this for me the way Sally did. When I needed to type my college term papers, Sally was there. When she called on the phone while I was out washing my car, she would ask, "Can I come over and help?" When I painted my parents' home, she was there—helping, serving, and making my life easier and more pleasant. She always observed me and watched for ways to help me.

Now, after thirty-seven years of marriage, this hasn't let up. It's gotten even better. Most people that visit us at our home feel I'm the most doted-over husband they've ever seen. I have to agree. No matter what Sally is doing, she is tuned in to me and is willing to give me a hand. She is truly a helper that is suitable for my personality, my needs, and my calling in life.

I don't have to worry about how the laundry and ironing are going to get done or when the bathroom is going to be scoured or what to plan for the menu. Sally takes care of all that. I empty the trash, help wash the dishes, and vacuum the house, but Sally runs the home smoothly, so that I can throw myself into the work God has called me to do.

Sally makes me look good. She works behind the scenes to enhance me and help me to be successful. Without Sally bringing balance to my personality and character, I would not be where I am today. We are like two Clydesdales, teamed up and working together to pull the wagon of life with all its duties, responsibilities, and challenges—and she is not a shirker. Rather, she goes the second mile—often!

Not everyone is like Sally and me, of course. I've met men who don't want their wives to dote on them like Sally does on me. Yeah, they like their wives to be there, and they want them to carry their share of the load in the marriage, but they like a more "hands-off" approach. The bottom line is that every successful marriage has to find a dynamic balance of responsibility and teamwork that matches who the husband and wife are and their circumstances in life.

I've met some women who expect their husbands to be their helpers and do double duty. In one attractive couple, both husband and wife pursued careers and seemed to get along well with each other—until baby number one came along. The wife quit her job and stayed home full time to raise her child. She found mothering to be all consuming and completely abandoned her household duties. Dishes piled up in the sink and on the counter. Dirty diapers stayed right where she dropped them when she changed her baby. Laundry and ironing didn't get done. She cuddled and played with her baby all day long.

When her husband came home from his job, she expected him to wash

Focused on Him

the dishes, do the laundry, clean the house, and take care of the baby, so that she could rest. By the time baby number three came along, the husband couldn't operate under this program any longer. They ended up divorcing.

Perhaps this is an extreme case, but if you find yourself on that end of the responsibility spectrum, God wants to help you find a better balance. God didn't design women to be dolls that need constant tending. Rather, He made them to be mature partners, willing to put their shoulder under real-life burdens. The Proverbs 31 woman develops good work habits, manages money well, and runs her household effectively. She looks for ways to relieve her husband of burdens and to enhance him. When this becomes your experience, you will find it a delight rather than drudgery.

Wives, study your man. What are his strengths and talents? What are his dreams and goals? What are his true heartfelt needs? What makes him feel loved and valued? What are the parts of God's design for him that he's not yet experiencing? Then ask yourself, "How can I be a true helper to my husband? How can I enhance his success in life?"

Why are Sally and I still "in love" after thirty-seven years of marriage? One simple reason is that I'm focused on Sally and Sally is focused on me. How about you? Wives, what's your focus? Is it primarily on yourself and your needs and wants—or is it on him?

Study Questions for Chapter 5

1. Do you know how to open your husband's heart?
2. Would your husband say you are focused on him?
3. How would your husband rate your marriage on a scale of one to ten? If you're not sure, ask him.
4. Would your husband say you are a Proverbs 31 wife?
5. Does your husband find you irresistible? If not, why not?
6. Does your husband see admiration and respect in your eyes?
7. Are you a real companion to your husband in the way he needs you to be?
8. Do you try to keep yourself attractive and dress as well as you did when you first met your man?
9. On a scale of one to ten, how would your husband rate your affections toward him?
10. In your husband's eyes, are you a daily helper to him?
11. What is God asking you to do to be number one in your husband's eyes and heart?

CHAPTER 6

Love Is Extravagant

> **God** demonstrates *His own love toward us,*
> *in that while we were* still sinners,
> *Christ* died *for us.*
> —Romans 5:8, *emphasis supplied*

J. D., Alecia, and I had been visiting for quite some time about the two marriage principles and how to implement them. I was amazed at the depth of their questions and comments. There was a thrill running through my emotional veins because here was a couple thinking it all through—at the outset of their marriage! The time passed quickly.

"So what's your next question?" I asked as Sally handed me a glass of water and then offered some to J. D. and Alecia.

J. D. took a drink, leaned forward with his elbows on his knees, and studied his glass of water before he looked up at me. "You said that if we implemented these two principles and were willing to pay the price, our love could just get better and better. I think we understand the two principles now. But what's the price we have to pay?"

I chuckled as I set my glass down on the nearby table. "Well, it's really quite simple. You will have what you value. If your marriage is not a priority, it will not remain irresistible. That's a cold, hard fact. Your marriage will be only as strong as what it costs to protect it. And the best protection I know is to invest in a little three-legged stool called *balance*."

The two lovebirds looked at me quizzically, so I continued. "The eroding process caused by everyday life in this world is real and never goes away. The devil has bound us with the galling yoke of a stressed, unbalanced, unprofitable, and busy life. You know what *busy* stands for, don't you? *Being Under Satan's Yoke.* In Christ's strength, we must break the devil's yoke and put on Christ's yoke which is restful, balanced, controlled, and purposeful.

"To enter into this lifestyle, you must continuously be evaluating the best use of your time for who you are and what you face. This involves continually adjusting the three legs of the stool to meet the changing stages and circumstances of life in order to maintain your God-directed balance."

"Well, tell us what those three legs are and what they have to do with a good marriage," Alecia interjected.

Finding balance

"The three legs are simplify, prioritize, and cultivate. You must live a life of simplicity so that you have time to devote to your priorities and to cultivate extravagant love. All three aspects are critical. If you try to prioritize and cultivate without simplifying, your little stool will fall over. Likewise, if you focus all your energy on living a life of simplicity without prioritizing your marriage or cultivating your relationships, you will also lose balance. Many people try to cultivate great relationships with God and their spouse without simplifying or prioritizing them, and they are continually frustrated and falling over, because the three legs must work together to balance the stool.

"The balance you need will vary according to your calling and the stage of life you are in. Moses spent forty years herding sheep and finding a real walk with God. Then he spent another forty years serving God's people. Both lifestyles were extremely different, but both were balanced for who and where Moses was at the time. Jesus spent thirty quiet years in Nazareth developing His character—then three-and-a-half active years in His ministry. Find balance for who and where you are.

"That balance must support irresistible love between the two of you, a love in which nothing is substituted for each other. You must hone your priorities and then give your best energies to cultivating them. The rest can wait, fall to the wayside, or be eliminated."

A very sober look came into J. D.'s and Alecia's eyes as the import of what I was saying began to soak in. "How do you do that in practical terms, Mr. Hohnberger?" J. D. asked. "Most people I know just kind of take life as it comes. They're always waiting for things to slow down so they can get around to what they think they should be doing."

"Your observations are very accurate, J. D. But that is the price to pay. You must decide to master your circumstances rather than allow them to master you.

"I'll get a pad of paper and show you how I sort out my priorities." I went to my desk and returned with a yellow pad and handed it to them. "Here's my list of priorities. I sort them out according to what is good, better, best, and a waste of time. Of course, some things are worse than a waste of time. Some things are downright evil. Those things went out when I accepted the Bible as my standard for life. But there are a lot of things in life that aren't evil but that will keep you from what is best—and that's where we so often get tripped up."

J. D. and Alecia studied my list:

Better and Best	**Good**	**Waste of Time**
Finding a daily walk with God	News, newspapers, magazines	News, newspapers, magazines
Making my wife my queen	TV and Radio	TV and Radio
Raising godly children	Internet and e-mails	Internet and e-mails
Touching others lives: Family Friends Church members Those in need	Social obligations	Competitive sports, hunting, and fishing
	Church duties	The party life and unprofitable social obligations
	Travel, vacation, and recreation	Mindless phone calls and empty meetings
	Professional career	Too much worldly success

After a moment, I continued. "For me, it's crucial that I identify, first of all, what is my top priority in view of the judgment and then analyze those things that compete for my attention. There are many good things that must have a place in our lives, but they can't become our lives. Most people have to work for a living, but when work becomes their life, they are out of balance. The same thing applies to our social involvements, church duties, travel, vacation, and recreation. Too much of a good thing crowds out those things that are better and best."

Alecia broke in. "You put some of the same things in both the 'good' and 'waste of time' columns. Was that a mistake?"

"No, that wasn't a mistake, Alecia. I put the news media in both columns for a reason. To me, burying myself in the daily trash, trouble, and trivia that the media churns out is a big waste of time. But neither do I advocate burying my head in the sand. If there is a hurricane brewing over Florida, and I'm planning to visit there, it would be prudent to know about it. Or if another war breaks out somewhere, you'd want to have an idea about what's going on. The principle is 'not never and not always.' You must continually filter through God what is the best use of your time and what is getting crowded out. If your top priorities are continually being shunted to the side, then you must refocus and redirect your energies. For me, my top priorities are not optional. They are essential. They are the practical expression of what Jesus meant when He said, ' "Seek first the kingdom of God and His righteousness." '[1]

"Good" in place of "best" becomes a "waste of time"

"I believe that for some people, Bible study could fit in the category of 'waste of time.' "

Alecia gasped. "How could that be? Isn't Bible study one of the top priorities?"

"Rightly pursued, Bible study is a vital part of learning to walk with God. But some people use it to avoid dealing with the real issues of their lives. It can become a substitute for a genuinely surrendered walk with God and an investment in their spouse and children. Jesus said it Himself. ' "You search the Scriptures, for in them you think you have eternal life; and these are they which testify of Me. But you are not willing to come to Me that you may have life." '[2]

Alecia looked at me like I was becoming heretical, so I explained further. "I have a friend I've known for years who is always coming up with some

---

1. Matthew 6:33.
2. John 5:39, 40.

'new light' regarding Bible prophecy for me to study. He can discuss the king of the north and the king of the south for hours on end and tell you all the latest developments concerning religious liberty. But his marriage is a mess, and he refuses to address it. His focus on end-time events has become a substitute for the work he needs to do in his own character and marriage."

"I think I see what you mean," Alecia responded. "When our Bible study keeps us from the better and best, it is out of balance."

"You got it!" I replied.

I looked at J. D. and could see the wheels turning in his head. "Mr. Hohnberger, it looks like sometimes you have to give up certain activities that are good and enjoyable—perhaps even permanently."

"Yes! That's right, J. D. If these activities displace your relationship with the one you married, they must either be eliminated as intruders or reprioritized to second, third, or fourth place. We all have only so much time, and it takes time to make our spouse a priority. So analyze your life, your time, and your priorities. Resolve to slow down. Learn to say 'No' gracefully. Draw a line eliminating the intruders and defending your top priority—and be prepared to take the heat."

"What do you mean by 'taking the heat'?" J. D. questioned.

"When I eliminated TV, the newspaper, magazines, sports, politics, and numerous social and church obligations to spend more time with my queen, my friends, relatives, and church members didn't understand. 'Jim, you're becoming fanatical,' they warned. 'You're a nut. You're not like us anymore.'

"But that's all right—because I'm in love at the age of sixty. I have weighed in the balances what I really care about. I have analyzed what is really worthy of my time. Or to put it another way, I have questioned what is really worthy of an overcommitment that crowds out a daily loving relationship with my wife. And I choose a new and better course."

"It sounds worth it to me!" Alecia piped up.

"Oh, it is," I continued. "You see, God's real purpose for us isn't all the fluff and peripheral things. It's having a real walk with Him, loving our spouses as He loves us, and then taking this attitude to the world. That is the full, successful life the world and the church are waiting to see.

"So define what in your life is evil, a waste of time, as well as what is good, better, and best. Then prioritize the best and better and drop all the rest. It's just that simple—but it's not very easy! We are *used* to living out our lives in the trifles, trash, trivia, and troubles this world presents to us. But we must break this pattern of low living if we are to keep our marriages irresistible. If we don't master these areas, they will master us.

"You may be afraid—as Stan was at first—that you will be deprived of what makes life worth living. Instead, you'll find the true purpose for living—relationships."

Alecia reflected, "It sounds a lot like getting off a junk food diet and starting an exercise program for the first time. It takes discipline and sticking to it if you want to feel better."

"That's a good comparison, Alecia. It *is* hard at first to learn to keep that little stool called *balance* level. But as you say 'No' to a thousand temptations and distractions, it becomes your lifestyle, and it gets easier. Jesus says, ' "Take up the cross, and follow Me." '[3] The cross is anything that needs to be eliminated from our daily habits and patterns of living to make time for the best God has to offer.

"Don't tire of the process. Just get good at it! Learn what God's expectations are for you in the present. Let others' expectations fall to the wayside. Then put your best energies into cultivating extravagant love."

Love extravagantly

I saw the stars in their eyes begin to twinkle again and Alecia asked, "What do you mean by 'extravagant love'?"

"I once came across a poem written by Joni Eareckson Tada that goes like this:

> Love is extravagant
> In the *price* it is willing to pay,
> The *time* it is willing to give,
> And the *strength* it is willing to spend.

"The word *love* has become a rather generic description for the things that bring us pleasure. We say things such as 'Oh, I just love my car.' 'I love chocolate chip cookies!' 'I love walking on the beach!' There is nothing wrong with this kind of love, so far as it goes—but that is not extravagant love. As the poem says, extravagant love is measured by the price you pay in your time and strength rather than by the level of your gratification."

"In other words," J. D. reflected, "it's what you *give* that counts more than what you *get*."

"Exactly! That's why Calvary is the greatest demonstration of extravagant love the universe has ever witnessed. Because there, God poured out all—everything—to redeem us. The price He paid was the life of His only

---
3. Mark 10:21.

begotten Son. Now, that's extravagant! Perhaps the most well-known text in all of the Scriptures is John 3:16, ' "For God so loved the world that He *gave*" ' " (emphasis supplied).

"You know, Mr. Hohnberger," Alecia said reverently, "I think that He not only *gave*—past tense—but He's still *giving* today."

"You're absolutely right, Alecia. And I think it is because He wants to reconnect us to Himself. The essence of heaven is life, love, and relationship. The essence of hell is death, alienation, and isolation. God wants to redeem us from the hellholes we create in our lives and give us a little taste of heaven on earth. And He cares about us so passionately that He was willing to lay down His very life.

"And that is what won my heart to Him. The reason I follow Christ is not so much that He has 'the truth,' but that He was willing to die for those who hated the truth—and that means me! At one time I wanted nothing to do with the Scriptures. They reproved my life and my ways. But when I saw God demonstrating His love toward me while I was yet a sinner, it turned my heart. That is why I follow Him—and as I do, He empowers me to do for Sally what He does for me—lavish her with extravagant love."

J. D. and Alecia studied me with a deepening earnestness and determination in their eyes. Yes, they would pay the price for an irresistible marriage. I continued.

"Christianity, true Christianity, is marked by a singleness of purpose, an indomitable determination, that refuses to yield to outward influences and aims at nothing short of God's standard and example. 'Lord, I'm following You. You are instilling in me the initial spark to redeem or initiate extravagant love in my marriage. Only by stepping out in faith and allowing Your daily grace to guide me step by step can I find that which is available to all who believe and follow after.'

"You remember the parable about the pearl of great price, don't you? ' "The kingdom of heaven is like a merchant seeking beautiful pearls, who, when he had found one pearl of great price, went and sold *all* that he had and bought it." '[4]

"That pearl of great price is Christ, and He is my most precious treasure. He is worth far more than anything I have to cut out of my life because it crowds Him out. He has become my source of extravagant love. And as I have found Him, I discovered another lovely pearl—the heart of my Sally."

Sacrifice is not enough

Later on, during the quiet evening hours, my reflections on extravagant

---

4. Matthew 13:45, 46, emphasis supplied.

love continued. *Is sacrifice,* I wondered, *enough, in and of itself?* My thoughts turned to 1 Corinthians 13:1–3. Here's my paraphrase of these verses:

> You can speak to your partner with the eloquence and appeal of angels, but without the investment of your heart, it just clangs in their ears. You can apply all your brilliance, wisdom, understanding, and faith to conquer every obstacle in your marriage, but without real love that links heart to heart, it amounts to nothing. And you can sacrifice all of your wealth, health, and even your life for your spouse—but unless your heart identifies and connects with your spouse's heart of hearts, you have missed the genuine sacrifice—and the genuine love of Calvary.

At Calvary, God did more than sacrifice the life of His precious, beloved Son. He forever identified Himself with us. He put Himself in our place—our place of weakness, vulnerability, helplessness, and isolation. He knows by experience what we feel. He enters into our joys, sorrows, and struggles. He is "touched with the feeling of our infirmities."[5] And it is out of this identification with us that He offers Himself to redeem us and reconnect us to Himself.

You can pour out good deeds and sacrifices for your spouse, but unless you give your heart as well, it is not extravagant love. I am to offer *myself* to my queen daily. My words are to open her ears; my actions are to speak so loudly they open her affections; my touch is to warm her heart. The gift of myself puts a smile upon her face. My time gives her the assurance of my extravagant love. It all says, "You are irresistible to me!" You see, love cannot last long without expression. So don't let your spouse's heart starve for lack of attention. Find out what their needs are. Place yourself in their shoes and empathize with their struggles. Pour yourself into ministering to them. Let them know that there is no sacrifice of your time and strength too great to make, no mountain too high to climb, no ocean too long to swim, no distance you won't travel to maintain the relationship you had at the beginning.

This isn't describing some sappy, Hollywood romance. This is real love, extravagant love, lived out by God's principles in the strength of Jesus Christ. You can't generate this kind of love. It comes only by having God's love shed abroad in your heart by the Holy Spirit.[6] It is a moment-by-moment transaction of filtering and listening and then acting as He prompts you to.

---

5. Hebrews 4:15, KJV.
6. See Romans 5:5.

Little everyday things

Extravagant love grows best through little attentions expressed often. It's not so much the big things in life that make the difference as it is the love expressed in little everyday things.

In our early years, Sally and I managed our toothpaste tube differently. She very carefully squeezed from the bottom, rolled up the empty part of the tube, and set it all neat and tidy in the medicine cabinet. I didn't want to be bothered with all that. I would just grab the tube, squeeze out some paste, and put the tube back in the most convenient-looking spot. You probably know just what kind of friction that produced!

Then there was our way of toweling off after a shower. Sally would stand inside the shower to dry herself off. She would carefully dry each foot before stepping out onto the bath mat and not splash a drop of water anywhere outside the shower. Not me! As soon as I turned off the faucet, I'd step right out onto the bath mat, grab my towel, and wipe myself down. Of course, by the time I was dry, the bath mat would be nearly drenched. Sally would come in a few minutes later in her stocking feet and step right on that wet bath mat. She would be furious, while I was oblivious!

Another source of friction was our perspective on punctuality. My father drilled into my head that if you're on time, you're late—and that included meals. Meals in my parents' home were always ready at least five minutes early. Sally's family was much more laid back about the whole mealtime thing. As long as the meal happened within fifteen or twenty minutes of the scheduled time, everything was fine. It was hard for her to understand why I got so uptight when she was still tossing the salad and setting the table at five minutes after the hour.

In each of these scenarios, we began to see a pattern for how we handled conflict. Sally would hold her anger inside, avoid confronting the behavior that bothered her, and rehearse the negative situation over and over in her mind. That only fostered alienation. On the other hand, I had no problem charging into conflicts with both barrels blazing.

We had to learn to go to Calvary and find there a willingness to do God's will rather than our own. I needed to tone down my overbearing approach, and Sally needed to honestly communicate her needs and desires. We needed to take turns speaking and listening.

In this way, we could find solutions for the little things that caused friction between us. I learned that it was a little thing to keep the toothpaste tube neatly rolled up and in its place in the medicine cabinet and to pick up the bath mat and hang it up to dry after I toweled off. Sally tackled learning, in Christ, how to have meals ready early instead of late. Sure, these were *little* sacrifices—

but they added up to *big* love, extravagant love!

The defining characteristic

Extravagant love visits Calvary as often as needed. In other words, my old thoughts and ways must be crucified so that the new marriage, in Christ, can come to life. This may be simple, but it is *not* easy. It requires that Christ's life be imparted daily through His Word and His Spirit. It requires a surrender of my old ways and a settling into His new ways. It means I must depend upon a *power* outside of myself the rest of my life. This is the Christian life. In discovering extravagant love for each other, you will be working out your own salvation in Christ and through His principles.

Extravagant love is the defining characteristic of God's presence in our lives and marriages. Let's take a look at the familiar passage of 1 Corinthians 13:4–7 to see how it expresses itself—and how it *doesn't* express itself. I like to lay the words out so I can see them. I've paraphrased some of the words based on Strong's definitions so I can better apply them to my marriage.

What Love Does	What Love Doesn't Do
Suffers long and is still kind	Envies—cherishes negative feelings
Expresses kindness in actions	Brags or boasts
Covers all things—endures the shortcomings of my spouse patiently	Puffs itself up
Believes all things—seeks to view circumstances and my partner through God's eyes rather than by what is apparent	Behaves rudely or in poor taste
Hopes all things—remains optimistic	Insists on a selfish perspective
Endures all things—doesn't give up	Becomes irritated

Never loses sight of its purpose of maintaining or regaining irresistibility	Dwells on the negative
Places a high value on what is good, right, and true—and communicates it	Glosses over destructive ways of relating

As I have thought about these characteristics, I've summarized them into three principles that keep extravagant love alive.

God's open-door policy

God's invitation to all of us is, " 'Come now, and let us reason together.' "[7] Wow! The God of the universe not only makes Himself available for reasoning together, but in the process allows for our perspective and individuality—as well as being tolerant of our shortcomings. Now that's quite a mouthful. Let's see if we can digest some of this extravagant love.

Right now, Alecia and J. D. can approach each other with just about anything. They are not only open to each other, but they are also tolerant of each other's varying perspectives. She's different than he is, and his extravagant love allows for her individuality. And hers allows for his. Wow—what love!

However, if either of them becomes self-oriented, the whole scenario changes. Suddenly, he doesn't have *time* for her "reasonings" and becomes intolerant of her perspective, which differs from his. Suddenly, he wants her to think and act just like he does. Her individuality now needs to be surrendered and smothered and become like his—or as he wants her to be. If not, she becomes a bother to him, a convenience only to be used for his needs and satisfaction. As a result, in time, the wonderful door to her heart closes. Why? Because self-love has taken over. This scenario can happen in reverse as well.

Note that in every relationship, even our relationship with the God of the universe, individual perspective is a quality of extravagant love. That does not necessarily mean that we agree on everything, but we allow the other person to have a different perspective. In other words, there is tolerance—not for evil, but for individuality. God has made no two people exactly the same.

---

7. Isaiah 1:18.

He doesn't believe in cookie-cutter cutouts, stamping out identical gingerbread men. No, each person has varying gifts, unique talents, different views, and IQs that range from low to extremely high. Some people are introverted, while others are extroverted. Some are entrepreneurs, and others are task oriented. Some love to express themselves, while others are content with only a few words.

So what am I saying? I'm saying that if God loves variety, let's not *stifle* the individuality in each other that He has created. I'm not talking about tolerating evil; I'm talking about giving each other the liberty to be and to discover the uniqueness of who he or she is and can become *in* Jesus through His Word. Marriage is a union of two lives, and should reflect both individuals—not just one or the other.

The apostle Paul wrote, "Where the Spirit of the Lord is, there is *liberty*."[8] If the Lord allows for such liberty, let us not squelch it in our loved ones. We must come to see the unique flower God has created in our spouses and then allow that flower—its fragrance, its petals—to bloom into all God intended for it to be. This Spirit in a marriage opens the door of the heart so it can thrive and not just survive.

Shortcomings

We all have shortcomings—one or more areas in our lives that come short of the expectations of our loved one. There is no perfect person. Jesus was the only balanced, perfect Person to walk this planet. Where we can, by God's grace, correct our shortcomings and level out our imbalances, let's do so. Let's not use as an excuse, "That's just the way I am." However, in this process of finding balance in Jesus, let's also be long-suffering with our spouse as Jesus is with us.

Let's enter into our spouse's struggles and try to understand what they feel and then do for them as we would have them do for us were we in their shoes. Let's be honest with each other about our downsides. But let's also realize that what one person finds very easy, another person may find very, very hard.

For example, I struggle with irritation, while Sally seems to have been born with a placid temperament. She struggles with overeating, while I can take or leave food. We vary; we are different. Where she is weak, I am strong. Where I am weak, she is strong. There is a growth curve for all of us. Let's learn patience and possess the long-suffering of God as we view these shortcomings in each other. This is extravagant love—a love that is worth possessing at the loss of all else. This extravagant love is available to everyone.

---

8. 2 Corinthians 3:17, emphasis supplied.

It's available to you—if you will pursue it with all your heart, all your mind, and all your soul. All may possess it, if all will pursue it.

While the process of developing this extravagant love is under construction, let's focus on each other's strengths. Let's see once again the gem we fell in love with and realize he or she may be a diamond in the rough. Let's see our spouses as they can be through God's polishing process and keep that ideal foremost in our thoughts, addressing problems where needed and staying focused on the solutions.

Little thoughtful attentions

I've already devoted three chapters of this book to the topic of expressing unselfish love to your spouse. But its importance can't be overstated. If you stay tuned to the heart of your partner in the little things, the big things will stay in line, too, in most cases.

To be honest, I find the little things that come up in life are often the bigger test of my sacrifice of time and strength—and yet they yield the most joy! My son, Matthew, began to understand this while he was dating Angela, the woman he eventually married.

Matthew and I had invited Matthew's best friend and his father to join us for our annual canoe voyage into the Quetico wilderness of Canada. We had taken this trip every year for a number of years, and Matthew looked forward to it as much as I did. But this year, he and Angela had begun to develop some closeness. He couldn't bear the thought of not seeing or talking to her for two weeks. Angela was facing some difficult challenges and was distraught over being apart from Matthew for so long—although she wouldn't hear of his not going on his favorite outing.

Matthew expressed his extravagant love by composing a special letter for each day he'd be gone. He called them Angela's "daily dose." The plan was that they would continue their daily connection through these letters. He labeled each one with the date it was to be opened, placed them all in a box, and gave them to Angela the evening before our departure. Her eyes glistened with tears as Matthew gave her that little box filled with his extravagant love. Then it was Matthew's turn to be surprised. Angela pulled out of her purse a little packet of letters in a waterproof bag for Matthew to open one at a time.

Matthew and Angela agreed to let us have a peek into their exchanges, and here's one of their letters.

"Searching for a Cell Phone" Letter 12
Dearest Angela,

Today I am overwhelmed with a quest for a way to talk with you. I got it, a cell phone! You know, that which I have forbidden Craig to bring along on such a trip in no uncertain terms. Boy, I sure wish he had brought it with him this time. But I have decided that the likelihood of someone else losing his or her cell phone on such a trip is possible. So the quest begins. I am driven on by an almost uncontrollable desire to talk with you. So I woke Craig up very *early* and briefed him about the important search of the day. As the break of dawn comes over the horizon, noiselessly, like professional, trained soldiers, we slip out of camp unbeknownst to the snoring sleeping guards on duty (the two fathers). In the canoe, we paddle stealthily away and up to our first portage. This is the most logical area for a cell phone to be lost in the shuffle of hoisting packs, grunting and exhaustion.

Disembarking at shore, we immediately begin searching the area with our noses to the ground. You see it is still quite dark yet! We traverse the entire portage looking under stumps and rocks, behind trees, amongst clumps of grass, and we run our hands deeply through every mud hole and puddle like raccoons in search of food. Remember, if someone lost one, you have to look in the most unlikely spots!

From one portage to another we travel, searching because my life is dependent upon it! Light dawns, the heat of the day is upon us, stomachs are empty and crying for food, but we press on still searching. We are miles away from camp, and the guards are definitely in a dither! Tiredness and hunger will not stop me! I must explore every option possible before I'll give up.

Evening is closing in upon us. I decide it is time to call in the FBI. The problem? I have no way to reach them! So I must resort to the FBI in my mind. We've searched portage, trail, hill, and swamp. We have only one other option—to search the bottom of the lakes! It is possible someone used a phone while fishing in a canoe and called his buddy to report the monster fish he caught. And as always is the case, pride comes before a fall, and while he is talking, the fish thrashes violently in the canoe, knocking his phone out of his hand and into the water. Yes, this is a possibility, so we must check. Diving into the water, we swim to the bottom searching more by hand than sight, because we have no goggles. Surfacing only when necessary, we dive and swim until we float to the top exhausted in front of our campsite. As "the guards" pull us ashore, I know I haven't succeeded, but I gave it my all. And yet I still dream that someone will drop one in my hand so I can hear your cheery voice. And so the cell phone quest ends.

Angela, you are more important to me than life itself! This time apart is hard, but it will only make us treasure our time together more in the future. I am thinking of you with all my heart! I love our time together and will never take a moment of it for granted in the future. I pray many times a day for you. Keep your spirits high!

Lovingly,
Matthew

It took time to write such extraordinary letters. There was a price to pay, but what joy there was in carrying it out! There was strength spent—but, oh, with such willingness of heart! Both Matthew and Angela looked forward every day to opening, reading, and digesting such extravagant love.

This is 1 Corinthians 13 love in action. Let's go back to that passage again, keeping in mind all that we have discussed about extravagant love, and this time, place Jesus' name in the place of the word *love*. Then read it as a prayer for your marriage that the power of God's love will be manifest in you and through your marriage in Jesus.

> *Jesus* suffers long and is kind; *Jesus* does not envy; *Jesus* does not parade *Himself,* is not puffed up; does not behave rudely, does not seek *His* own, is not provoked, thinks no evil; does not rejoice in iniquity, but rejoices in the truth; bears all things, believes all things, hopes all things, endures all things. *Jesus* never fails.[9]

When this quality of Christ's love is the focus of our everyday lives, then its virtue will make us "irresistible again" regardless of our age or our past failures. This should be the all-consuming force of our lives every day until we see Jesus.

Which path are you on?

So, the price to pay is high. You must simplify your life, prioritize your marriage, and cultivate extravagant Calvary love. Many people consider the price too high. But those who pay the price have no regrets.

Like Bud and Paula. This couple are close friends of Sally and me; we have watched their family for nearly twenty years. Bud is a head mechanic

---

9. 1 Corinthians 13:4–8, personal paraphrase.

for John Deere, and Paula is a housewife and mother. Early in their marriage, before their two girls were born, they bought one acre of land on a little knoll in grain country. They built an attractive, yet simple, 1,600-square-foot, three-bedroom, one-bath home that they heat with wood. Their electrical needs are supplemented with solar power, and their grocery bill is kept down by the garden they plant. They've never owned a TV or a fancy car. They raised and homeschooled two lovely girls. Bud and Paula claim they have never had an argument, and they always have time for each other.

At one time, a friend encouraged Bud to open his own mechanic business in the shop he built on his one acre. He did—and life got complicated. Clients started showing up at all hours of the day. Bookwork pressed him for time; phone calls demanded his attention. He couldn't leave on vacation, because people counted on him. The added stress so affected their time and energies that Bud went back to his former employment.

Today Bud and Paula are two of the people I most respect. Why? Their relationship with each other has not just survived—it has thrived. They have paid the price for extravagant love, and it has made their home a joyful little heaven on earth.

I can't help but compare the home of Bud and Paula to that of Jerry and Vicki—another couple with whom we've been friends for years. Jerry and Vicki really loved each other. They were well matched and tied the knot in their late twenties. But Jerry and Vicki chose different priorities. Jerry wanted Vicki and other people to look up to him. He started two businesses—both of which were extremely successful. So successful, in fact, that he'd often work until midnight. Vicki was highly involved in church and community causes.

Jerry and Vicki also had two children, but Jerry had no time for them other than a token amount here and there. Instead of investing himself in Vicki and his children, Jerry invested himself in material possessions and gave them to his family. He built Vicki a grand home and spared no expense. She had a maid to clean the house, a cook to help with the elaborate dinners they threw for his business clients and her social causes, a classy sports car to drive when she went shopping, a luxurious vacation rental, and anything else she might want.

Jerry and Vicki have grown apart over the years and now, in their fifties, they have a mere coexistence. It breaks my heart to say it, but their home is just the opposite of heaven on earth. It has become a "hell"—blazing with the fire of contention and icy with the chill of alienation. They have little in common and no romantic life. Vicki has threatened divorce numerous times.

Both of these couples had their priorities, but their priorities differed. Jerry and Vicki got caught up in materialism and success. However, their definition of success was prominence and wealth, whereas Bud and Paula defined success as their love relationship with each other. There is a cost both ways. It just depends on what you're willing to sacrifice. Jerry and Vicki are at the ending point of their relationship, whereas Bud and Paula are irresistibly in love.

Which will it be for you?

> Love is extravagant
> In the price it is willing to pay
> The time it is willing to give
> And the strength it is willing to spend.

Study Questions for Chapter 6

1. Would your spouse say your love is extravagant?
2. Are you willing to pay the price for such love?
3. Are you willing to give the time to secure such love?
4. Are you willing to spend the strength to develop such extravagant love?
5. What sacrifice is God asking you to make to revitalize your marriage?
6. Do you feel the greatest gift—extravagant love—is worth the necessary price in time and strength?
7. Is there an "open-door policy" in your marriage?
8. What are you going to do with your spouse's shortcomings?
9. Will you give your spouse thoughtful attentions based on his or her needs?

CHAPTER 7

Love Killers

*Catch all the foxes,
those little foxes,
before they ruin the vineyard of love,
for the grapevines are blossoming!*
—Song of Solomon 2:15, NLT

Do you get the picture? You've planted a vineyard of extravagant love. You've prioritized it, cultivated it, nurtured it—and now it's beginning to blossom. Then the little foxes get in. They dig for rodents and disrupt the fragile roots; they gnaw on the tender shoots and break the branches. In a short time, your lovely vineyard is ruined.

Every couple has to deal with the little foxes. Stan and Susan did. They had to replant their vineyard and learn to protect it from the little things that destroy love in a big way. Bill and Barbara did too. And so did Sally and I. Hopefully, J. D. and Alecia will "catch all the foxes, those little foxes, before they ruin the vineyard of love."[1]

Over the years, as Sally and I have cultivated our own vineyard of love and helped hundreds of other couples to do the same, we've seen the same little foxes showing up again and again. We call them "love killers" and have classified them into five categories:

1. Selfishness
2. Ineffective communication
3. Lack of boundaries
4. Strained finances
5. "I can't" or "I won't"

If you learn to spot these five "little foxes" early, you can shoo them away before they ruin your vineyard. Or if the damage has already been done, it's

---

1. Song of Solomon 2:15, NLT.

still not too late to deal with them. Let's look at each of these five in turn.

Selfishness

Selfishness is a sly little fox that creeps into your vineyard under a thousand different disguises. You can recognize it by a subtle change in your willingness to sacrifice for your spouse. Instead of focusing on *us,* you begin to focus on *me;* you stop adapting to the needs and wishes of your spouse. He or she is significant to you only to the degree that you are benefited.

Henry Cloud has written, "When one is self-centered, he guarantees the failure of love, for love is an attachment between two people, and the self-centered person denies the reality of the 'other.' He only sees others as extensions of himself. They exist to make him happy, serve his needs, and regulate his feelings or drives in life."[2]

This dynamic on the part of one or both partners is a *big* warning sign. Sally and I didn't see it coming. While we were courting, Sally's dreams, hopes, desires, and needs got my full attention. I was there for her—and she was there for me. We corralled every moment that we could into spending time with each other.

Then we got married, and Sally, a registered nurse, took a job on the evening shift. I was bored, so I developed replacements for Sally. My buddies, TV, sports, news, hunting, and business slowly but imperceptibly captured my attention. I didn't stop loving Sally, but I loved her in conjunction with my many other interests, and a subtle shift took place. Instead of continuing to actively pursue her affections, I let her become simply a convenience—something to make my life easier, someone who would serve my needs and make me happy. And when she didn't meet my expectations, she tasted my displeasure. Sally bent over backward to try to please me, but her heart went into hiding.

That little fox did quite a bit of damage before God was able to get our attention. It was quite a process for us to reverse things. Sally had to risk sharing her honest needs, wishes, and concerns; I had to learn to see her again as an individual—not just an extension of myself.

That's when God planted a transforming principle in my life. It goes like this: if something is very important to your spouse—and it doesn't violate biblical principle—*do it!* As a Christian, you are supposed to be living to serve, not to be served. Christ and all of heaven live to minister to the fallen human race. Lay aside your "I don't want to" and live to please your loved one.

For example, Sally had been flipping through a garden catalog, when a white picket fence caught her eye. She stared at it for a while, and a vision

---

2. http://www.cloudtownsend.com/library/articles/7articles1.php.

began to form in her mind. She could see that fence over in one corner of our front yard with flowers blooming all around it. The longer she thought about it, the more beautiful the vision became. When she looked out our front window, that corner of the yard seemed bare and boring without a white picket fence. She tore out the page of the catalog and placed it on my side of the desk.

The next time I was going through my papers, I saw what she had circled for me to look at. I didn't like it, so I put it back on her side of the desk and promptly forgot all about it.

But the next year, Sally saw the same picket fence in a catalog, and she liked it even more the second time. So she tore out the page and put it on my side of the desk again. This time, I asked her about it. "Sally, do you really like this white picket fence?"

"Oh, I do, Jim!" she answered enthusiastically.

"Well, where would it go?" I asked, looking out the front window.

"Oh, I thought it could go over there in the corner with a flower bed in front of it. It would be such a lovely accent in our yard! Besides, I've always wanted a white picket fence."

I frowned. This was slightly irritating. "Well, Sally, if we lived in the city where you need something to look at, you'd have your white picket fence. But we live in the wilderness. We have the Rocky Mountains to look at. This fence idea would be a distraction and a nuisance. I'd have to mow around it and weed the flower bed and trim it and water it—I don't think it's reasonable."

We dropped the conversation, but it came up again—and again and again. Sally kept bringing up such things as the importance of her "individuality" and what a bargain the price was and that the cost fit in our budget and that she'd always wanted just such a fence and wouldn't I reconsider. But every time I thought about it, it just made no logical sense to me.

Then one morning as I was praying, the white picket fence came up in my mind. *"Jim,"* the Lord asked, *"is the white picket fence immoral?"*

No, Lord.

"Would it strain your budget?"

No, Lord.

"Is it so repulsive to you that you absolutely could not live with it?"

Well, I guess not, Lord.

"Does it violate any other biblical principle that you know about?"

Hmm. No, Lord.

"Then why don't you sacrifice what you think is 'common sense' and 'logic' and let Sally have her white picket fence?"

At that point, I recognized that clinging to my own perspective would be selfishness, and I had a choice to make.

When Sally sat down at the breakfast table that morning, her eyes grew real big. There on her plate was the oft-discussed catalog page with a big note taped to it. "Buy it, honey! I love you! ❤"

To be honest with you, I still don't like that white picket fence. To me, it's an eyesore. But I love my Sally, and I cherish the joy I find in treasuring her above my own egocentric opinion.

This war against selfishness is not "once conquered—always conquered." You've got to enter into the battle daily. That's why Paul says, "I die *daily*."[3] This little fox is always lurking—just waiting for a chance to do some damage. Without a daily life of faith and surrender, our love will turn the corner and begin living for itself rather than for the other.

Another way selfishness weasels its way into our relationships is through the idea that things have got to be fair. Now it might seem that "playing fair" would be a good thing—but it wreaks havoc in marriages. After all, the concept of an " ' "eye for an eye and a tooth for a tooth" ' "[4] is based on the idea of fairness. Fairness says, "If you're nice, I'll be nice. If you hurt me, I'll hurt you back."

Bill and Barbara were caught up in this thinking. "You know what Bill does?" Barbara mulled over in her mind. "He gives me this icy cold shoulder all week long, and then at church he's warm and flirty with the other women. Then he has the audacity to complain that I'm not excited about making love to him. So I'll show him. Every time I buy gas, Frank leans over the counter and asks me how I'm doing. He seems genuinely interested in me. And the last time I saw him, he invited me to have lunch with him. I think I'll take him up on it. Under the circumstances, I think that would be fair."

Of course, when Bill found out what Barbara was up to, did he think, "Oh, that makes sense. She's only playing fair"? Of course not! To him, Barbara's actions were a low blow, so it was only fair, in his mind, that he protect his tender feelings by withdrawing even more, all the while complaining about Barbara's inadequacies as a wife. And so the game progressed.

Listen to what Jesus says, " 'But if you love those who love you, what credit is that to you? For even sinners love those who love them. And if you do good to those who do good to you, what credit is that to you? For even sinners do the same.' "[5]

Every relationship has its problems, and no spouse is perfect. If you oper-

---

3. 1 Corinthians 15:31, emphasis supplied.
4. Matthew 5:38.
5. Luke 6:32, 33.

ate on the idea that everything must be fair and balanced, then the lowest behavior becomes the highest standard. Rise above this thinking. "Do not be overcome by evil, but overcome evil with good."[6]

More often than not, your willingness to sacrifice what's "fair" and instead seek God to learn how to truly love your spouse will bring about a similar response in your mate—or at least it will open up communication about why they did what they did.

This brings us to the second of the "little foxes" we must keep from destroying the vineyard of our marriage relationship.

Ineffective communication

Quite often, communication deteriorates following marriage—either because we don't give it priority, we are no longer motivated, or because we lack communication skills. With that in mind, we need to take a proactive approach. This means that you need to set aside time every day for some one-on-one connecting and then work at developing effective communication between the two of you.

Sally and I typically do this twice a day. At noon, we sit down together for a half hour on the swing in front of our house. We call that our "swing time." And in the evening, we take a walk together for about half an hour. No, we aren't able to do this every single day—but missing it is the exception rather than the rule.

Sometimes during our talk times, we have differences or misunderstandings to work out. Other times, we connect about upcoming plans or schedules and how we will work together. Sometimes, we just share how our day is going or reflect gratefully about our lives together.

During this time, we try to create a sense of safety in which each feels free to share openly without being judged or interrupted. We want to connect heart-to-heart, and that means we need to listen beyond the words the other person is speaking and try to understand the intent of his or her heart. That's what we did when we were courting each other, and we try to keep it alive in the present.

Each person needs to understand his or her strengths and weaknesses. Some talk too much and too loudly and find it easy to make harsh, belittling comments. Others are too quiet and easily intimidated. They express agreement when they'd really like to disagree, but fear conflict. Know who you are and temper or strengthen your natural personality in the Lord. Listen to your conscience and do what God is asking you to do. Learn to identify those crafty little foxes that derail communication and send them packing.

---

6. Romans 12:21.

Here are some of the ones we've encountered:

Dredging up the past. Some people feel they must work out everything that's happened in the past before they can move on—but that approach will almost always derail you. Leave the past alone—especially during the first ninety days of turning your marriage around.

Try to establish a new present. If something from the past remains unresolved, it will show up in the present. Then deal with it in the present, referring to the past only for the purpose of gaining insight to solve the present issue.

Both spouses should communicate their perspectives without attacking the other person, arguing, interrupting, or sidetracking.

If emotions begin to rise and a problem becomes too difficult to work through, agree to table it until you've had time to gain a fresh perspective. Then prayerfully try again. If that doesn't resolve the problem, ask someone with depth of experience and spirituality to arbitrate or counsel. If that doesn't solve it, agree to disagree.

Arguing over problems. When problems come up—and they will—spend 5 percent of your time stating the problem from your perspective and 95 percent offering a creative solution. Stay on the solution. See yourselves as a team, united to solve the problem in front of you, rather than as adversaries dueling over a problem between you.

Most couples spend 95 percent of their time arguing over the problem. "You did this!" "No, I didn't!" "Yes, you did!" "I did not!"

Pretty soon, you are so mad at each other you can hardly remember what the problem even was in the beginning! Instead of the issue being a problem needing a creative solution, your partner becomes the enemy. This pattern must be reversed!

Pray together and ask God for wisdom. Study the issue in the context of Scripture and be willing to apply biblical principles. Ask others you respect how they solved a similar problem. Stay solution-oriented. Always remember: your spouse is not your enemy!

Refusing to see your part in the problem. It's often easier to see your spouse's part in the problem than your own, but the inability to see and admit your own behavior—especially when you are wrong—can stall a relationship as fast as anything I know. No relationship or person is perfect, but you can work through any kind of conflict as long as both people involved are able and willing to look at their own behavior and admit it. When one or both parties are unable or unwilling to do that, the marriage gets stuck.

The Bible says, "If we say that we have no sin, we deceive ourselves, and the truth is not in us."[7] Always be willing to examine yourself to see what

---

7. 1 John 1:8.

you are contributing to the problem. Deal with yourself first and then work toward a solution with your mate.

Detaching emotionally. As I looked at J. D. and Alecia across the living room, they were anything but emotionally detached! They were connecting—not just with their minds—but also with their hearts. They freely shared their innermost feelings, fears, vulnerabilities, and dreams. The result was irresistible intimacy—"in-to-me-you-see"!

But what happens when spouses detach themselves emotionally? The lights are on, but nobody is home. Each starts to feel "out of touch" with the other, and in the best scenario, a shallow relationship results. In the worst, the two grow further and further apart until the marriage dies.

God wants us to love Him with our hearts as well as our minds. That means He values our feelings as well as our thoughts. Getting in touch with our emotions and expressing them to our spouse allows our mate to "know" us and creates closeness.

I grew up in a stoic German family that did not easily share inner feelings and vulnerable emotions. I have had to learn in adulthood to communicate on that level with Sally. I used to think she wouldn't respect me if I shared my emotions and feelings, but I've discovered the contrary. She feels drawn to me—and I to her!

Lobbying. Some spouses operate like lawyers lobbying for their causes. They have their pet issues, and they watch for every opportunity to win their case. The problem is that the marriage loses. A marriage relationship is about "us"—not about "me versus you."

Instead of lobbying to win and get what's best for you, ask God to show you what's best for the marriage. Give your mate the security of knowing that you are in the marriage for both of you—not just for your own interests.

"You should . . ." Husbands and wives are meant to be equals and share their lives in a spirit of mutuality. When one attempts to dominate the other with an attitude of "I know better," communication and the relationship deteriorates. In this scenario, one partner behaves more like a parent than a spouse. You tend to hear a lot of "you shoulds" as the dominating partner freely tells the other person how to think, live, be, and act.

The person being dominated feels belittled, controlled, disrespected, and often resentful. Their drive to find freedom from domination often furthers the alienation.

Love and effective communication can flourish only where genuine respect for the freedom and rights of both individuals are valued. Christ died to guarantee us freedom of choice. How must He feel when we attempt to rob our spouses of that very freedom by refusing to honor their rights as a separate individual, free to do what they want with what is their own?

Giving up. All skills take practice to improve, and effective communication is no exception. Let your partner see a willingness in your style and approach. Don't give up, and in time you will settle into a communication pattern that works for you. Then work it and grow in it continually for the rest of your lives.

Lack of boundaries

This is the third of the little foxes threatening your marriage. When I was putting together the content for this chapter, my personal assistant suggested that "lack of boundaries" was a significant love killer in marriage. My first reaction was, "What do boundaries have to do with marriage?"

She responded, "They have a lot to do with marriage. The vast majority of marriages suffer from unresolved boundary issues and could benefit from addressing them."

As I thought more about it, I realized that boundaries in a relationship have everything to do with keeping love alive because proper boundaries preserve the essential ingredients of freedom, individuality, and responsibility.

In real estate, boundaries describe property lines and define ownership. If I own a house with a yard, I am responsible for what is inside my "boundaries." If my lawn needs to be watered, and the weeds need to be pulled, I'm responsible for seeing that these jobs get done. On the other hand, my responsibility ends with my property line. I don't have the right to climb over the fence into my neighbor's yard and start cleaning up his garden. I can offer him my help, and he can open his gate and let me in if he chooses. But it's his choice.

Likewise, in a relationship, boundaries tell you where you begin and end and what you are responsible for. Our thoughts, feelings, attitudes, behaviors, choices, limits, desires, values, talents, and love all lie within our property lines. When we accept responsibility for cultivating these things and allow or require our mates to do the same, we find the freedom to truly love.

Boundary problems are usually seen in someone's inability either to say "No" when they need to, or to hear "No" from others. Consequently, we either allow people to walk all over us in a way that destroys respect, or we walk all over them and "trespass" against them, destroying love in the process. True love respects each other's boundaries, saying "No" when we need to, and respecting it when we hear it.

Gina had a hard time knowing her own limits, and Roy had a hard time respecting them. Roy expected Gina to serve him a hot meal anytime he wanted it, and he refused to be regulated by a schedule. He might get up at

5:00 A.M. one day and expect pancakes and hash browns by 6:00—and a well-packed, homemade lunch ready to go out the door. Or he might just as well sleep in until 8:00 and eat around 9:00 A.M. Gina spent many years catering to his whims until God impressed on her heart the conviction that she needed a regular time in the morning to pray, study, and exercise. She also needed to follow a predictable schedule with their three school-age children.

For a long time, Gina hesitated to make a change, because she feared the wrath of her husband. She believed the fallacy that she was responsible for Roy's anger and that she must please him in order to keep the anger in check. However, it never seemed to work. No matter how hard Gina tried to please Roy, he still became angry when something crossed his wishes. She felt victimized by his anger, because she also believed that he was responsible for making her happy by approving of her.

Do you see how both Gina and Roy were crossing boundaries and expecting the other to care for things that belonged on their side of the fence—namely their emotions and happiness?

As Gina continued to pray and study, the conviction that she needed more order in her life deepened, and finally she took a step. First, she approached Roy with the need for a schedule. He brushed her aside saying, "Look, if you expect me to bring home my paycheck, I expect to have my meals when I want them."

Gina was a bit shaken by that repulse and went back to God. Had she been mistaken? No, she still sensed God asking her to cultivate regularity. Prayerfully, she planned a regular time each morning to serve breakfast that would allow her to spend consistent time with God each morning and have a predictable routine for the children. If Roy needed breakfast early for some reason, he would need to let her know the day before so she could have something in the oven or Crock-Pot for him. If he planned to eat later than the rest of the family, he could reheat the food.

Roy was angry when Gina told him her plan. Gina struggled with a lot of guilt feelings, and Roy wrestled with thoughts of blame. But in time, Roy respected Gina for the stance she had taken and found the regular schedule benefited him too. He actually became its chief defender! Gina learned that she could love Roy more when she wasn't compelled to do so by feelings of fear or guilt. Their marriage grew with their increasing sense of personal responsibility and freedom in Christ.

This example illustrates another aspect of boundaries: requiring responsible behavior from each other in a relationship and taking a stand against those little foxes when they intrude their cunning faces. True love cannot grow when evil is allowed to triumph. When we establish boundaries to "abhor what is evil,"[8] and take a stand against it, we preserve the good in a relationship and help it to grow by solving problems.

If this concept is unfamiliar to you, I highly recommend the books *Boundaries* and *Boundaries in Marriage* by Henry Cloud and John Townsend.[9] The principles they present are both biblical and extremely practical in sorting out relational issues.

Strained finances

Financial conflict is one of the top reasons many marriages end in divorce. And even for those marriages that stay intact, lack of unity in financial decisions can be an area of contention that eats away at their heart. Don't let this "little fox" get the best of you!

Society has programmed us to believe that houses, cars, furniture, clothing, sporting goods, and other possessions bring happiness and that it's OK to leverage your bank account in order to be happy. The rather startling fact is that the average person in America spends $1.10 for every dollar earned.[10] Someone has said, "When your outgo exceeds your income, your upkeep becomes your downfall!" By trying to get more and more of this world, we have less and less of each other and God. Soon we find our lives and finances spiraling out of control.

The first solution most of us turn to when facing financial problems is to try making more money, and some couples do need to qualify themselves to earn an adequate income. But more often than not, poor management and materialistic goals are the real cause of fiscal trouble; simply making more money won't solve the problem. We must address our underlying attitudes and beliefs about money. *How* we manage our finances is often a greater key to our financial stability than the *amount* of money we make.

God cares about your finances and intends them to be a blessing. Everything we own belongs to Him. The possessions we have are a trust from God, and He expects us to be good stewards of them. The Bible contains 2,350 verses about handling money and possessions. One of them says, "A little that a righteous man has is better than the riches of many wicked."[11]

When Sally and I were dating, I used to have her cut my hair because I didn't have the money to visit a barber. But it didn't matter to us. We had each other, and we were wonderfully in love! After we got married, we pursued the

---

8. Romans 12:9.
9. Published by Zondervan and available in bookstores everywhere.
10. According to Howard Dayton, *Your Money Map* (Chicago: Moody Publishers, 2006), 118.
11. Psalm 37:16.

riches of this world and lost each other's extravagant love. Which was better?

We learned the hard way not to get caught in the trap of overextended finances. Debt becomes a galling yoke that creates stress and arguments. It's better to downsize than oversize. Stay far away from the myth of the "American Dream"! Concentrate on your relationship and be content with a "little" that a righteous man has. If you can't be content with what you have, you won't be happy with what you want either.

Educate yourselves on God's principles for financial management. Couples who commit to learning about their spending tendencies and who work together on their financial plan—whether spending, saving, giving, or investing—actually find their marriages strengthened. Delving into this topic in-depth is beyond the scope of this book, but there are some excellent materials available to help you do that. One source I highly recommend is Crown Financial Ministries.[12]

Achieving financial freedom requires discipline and planning, but it is well worth the effort to protect and support your marriage. True happiness, joy, and peace come from the connecting of two hearts together—not the abundance of possessions and an easy life.

"I can't" or "I won't"

Of all the little foxes that chew away at your vineyard of love, none do more damage than this one. This "little fox" is all about attitude. If two married people have the attitude "I can do all things through Christ who strengthens me,"[13] the difficulties posed by selfishness, ineffective communication, boundary issues, and strained finances will serve to propel them forward. Two people committed to owning, facing, and dealing with the challenges in their marriage, are going to grow.

That's why I believe that adaptability is one of the most important attributes to look for when considering a spouse. Marriage brings two different lives together. Two different family governments. Two different perspectives. It can't be all one way!

This understanding isn't easy for many individuals. Selfishness, stubbornness, pervades, and this must be surrendered. On all issues not involving biblical principles, there must be a willingness to work out creative alternatives that both spouses will adhere to throughout their married life.

Serious self-evaluation must take place, letting God's Word speak to you and His Spirit lead you. All rigidity must be laid aside. A willingness to consider the other's perspective is a must on a continuous basis.

---

12. www.crown.org.
13. Philippians 4:13.

All couples have differences. That is a given. But what they do with these differences determines whether they will be successful together in their married life.

If one or both spouses adopt the attitude "I can't" or "I won't," the marriage will stall and get stuck. Many couples live their whole lives stuck—which generally means stale. And they can stay very busy maintaining their stalled condition. But they miss out on the great potential that God has for them in life—irresistible love. Each may have a wish to grow, but they wait for the other to take the first step—and so they stay stalled. No one changes. They just live in an uncomfortable familiarity. But God says, "Because they do not change, Therefore they do not fear God."[14]

If you are saying "I can't" or "I won't," you are saying "I'm in charge." That means you are man-managed rather than God-governed, and you are not safe to bring into God's kingdom.

Being stalled is not really the problem, however. It is a *symptom* of the problem. The underlying attitude—"I can't" or "I won't"—is really the problem that paralyzes the marriage from moving forward.

"I won't" is an attitude of complacency based on selfishness, rigidity, or pure slothfulness. It says, "I like where I am, and I won't budge! I don't feel like investing the time and energy to make our marriage irresistible."

If that's you, you must be willing to be made willing. In Christ's strength, you must lay down your negative-reactive thoughts and emotions and replace them with proactive "can do" thoughts and emotions.

Sometimes complacency is comfortable because the nail is not long enough. What do I mean by that?

A man was visiting a ranch one hot, sultry day and noticed a dog lying in a shady spot on the edge of the porch. The dog had a peculiarly uncomfortable look in his expression and posture. The man commented on this to the rancher, and the rancher said, "Oh, that's because the spot he's lying on has a big nail sticking up in the middle of it."

"Why doesn't the dog just move?" the visitor logically reasoned.

The rancher thought a moment and then drawled, "I guess the nail isn't long enough."

Sometimes God allows circumstances to "lengthen the nail" to motivate us to move out of our familiar ruts. If that's you and you sense that things aren't going too well in your life and relationships, it could be that God is trying to lovingly nudge you to a better place. To move forward, you must be willing to live on the principles of God's Word and Jesus' life in us—not your emotions and feelings.

---

14. Psalm 55:19.

The sister to "I won't" is "I can't." "I won't" is anchored in complacency, but "I can't" is usually motivated by fear. Perhaps the "I can't" individual stepped out and ventured something in the past, and it turned out badly. Perhaps he or she fears getting burned again. "I can't" seems so true to such an individual.

In one sense, the "I can't" person is right. That's why he or she needs God, as we discussed in chapter 2. God is the Fountain of wisdom, strength, and courage. Drawing from His grace, the "I can't" person can find the courage to answer His call, to face fear, step into new paths, and try again.

It's not God's will for any of us to stay stuck in complacency or fear. He has sufficient grace for anyone who will take hold of His hand and walk with Him one step at a time. So what happens when one partner in a marriage gains the vision of irresistible love, takes God's hand, and begins to move forward—but the spouse says, "No, I don't want to. I don't know how. I can't"?

What do you do when your marriage is stalled? We'll look at that question in the next chapter.

Study Questions for Chapter 7

1. Which of the "little foxes" described in this chapter is ruining your vineyard of love?
2. Do you respect your spouse as an individual separate from yourself or do you see him or her as an extension of yourself to meet your needs and desires?
3. In what ways do you "play fair"?
4. Is your communication mostly ineffective or effective?
5. Do you spend more of your time arguing over the past and your problems rather than dealing with the present and solutions?
6. Is it hard for you to say "No" when you need to? Is it hard for you to hear "No" from your spouse?
7. Do both of you require responsible behavior from each other in order to protect your relationship from "the little foxes"?
8. Are you master of your finances or have your finances mastered you?
9. Can you recognize either complacency or fear holding you back from taking the steps God is asking you to take in your marriage?
10. When are you going to begin dealing with the "little foxes" in your marriage?

CHAPTER 8

Stalled

Let him know that he who turns a sinner from the error of his way will save a soul from death and cover a multitude of sins.
—James 5:20

There they were again—the same couple I had noticed at two previous meetings. As I was preaching, they stood out to me from the rest of the audience for some reason. It could have been the fact that they were a very attractive couple, but I think it was more the contrast in their attitudes that caught my attention. She hung on every word I was saying, took notes, and responded with smiles, nods, and amens at the appropriate times. She was with me all the way through the sermon.

His demeanor was quite the opposite. He avoided making eye contact with me and often seemed to be sending or receiving text messages on his cell phone while I talked. He had a bored look about him that said, "I'd rather be anywhere but here."

As soon as the meeting ended, I made my way over to them. She readily introduced herself as Nancy and her husband as Todd. In person, I sensed the same contrast as I had from the pulpit. She was warm, responsive, and engaging. He was cold, reserved, and distant—which kept our conversation from getting very far.

Later, as Sally and I walked back to our cabin, we found Nancy waiting for us on a park bench beside our path. "Could I talk to you two for a moment?" Her face was tear-stained.

"Sure, we have a few minutes now. And if that's not enough, we'll schedule more time tomorrow." Sally and I sat down beside her, and her story tumbled out—a story we've heard repeated all too often by both husbands and wives.

One partner catches the vision for an irresistible marriage, and he or she wants to go for it. It's worth fighting for! Change is welcome. The other partner, however, doesn't share these feelings. The other spouse is content to be stalled. "Don't rock my boat; I'm not budging."

But marriage is a partnership between two people, so if one refuses to budge, the other is doomed to stay stalled, right? Not necessarily.

Marriage is a *dynamic* partnership—sort of like kids on a seesaw. What one spouse does has an effect on the other. You can't change how your partner rides his side of the seesaw, but you *can* change what you do on your side. And as you tune into God's directions for how He would have you ride your side, it will affect your partner's ride. Then he or she has to choose how to respond.

I do not believe there is only one way to redeem marriages. God has a thousand ways of correcting wrong courses. I don't pretend to know all of them. However, I have observed five avenues within which God works in different ways to bring out a new life within your marriage! So if your spouse is not motivated, is too laid back, self-centered, has other interests, or is involved with immorality, please prayerfully consider with the Lord and His Word these five steps that you can take to bring about change. Remember that the objective is to *restore* your loved one—not to rebuke, reprove, or push him or her away.

Outside help

1. A godly support team. When you decide to take steps to move a stalled marriage off of dead center, you are risking loss for the sake of gain. Your connection with your mate may not be a positive one, but it is one you have learned to count on. When you begin to change, the threat of being abandoned or isolated by your mate is very real. Nothing guarantees that they have to keep riding the seesaw. They may just walk away. Or they may try a number of tactics to pressure you into maintaining the old ways.

In either case, you need sources of love and connection other than your spouse to strengthen you to take the hard steps of tough love that will give your marriage a chance to become irresistible. Don't try to do it alone.

God is your primary support base. Remember what we discussed in chapter 2? That's always our starting point. God is the Source of all that you need, and you can trust Him fully. He can supply you with strength, wisdom, opportunities, direction, comfort, healing, forgiveness, ability, love, hope, courage, principles, and many other things. He has a thousand ways to provide for you that you know nothing about. So open your heart to Him. Connect with Him. Allow Him to work out His will in your life.

God often works through His body—the church—to provide the support we need. Paul compared the church to a body with Christ as the Head.

Each member of the body has a part to play in supporting and helping the other parts of the body. So as you lean on God for support and direction, watch for the opportunities He provides to connect with people who will support you in your goal of moving your marriage off of dead center.

You need people who will be "for" your marriage—not blind to the changes that need to happen, but also not eager to throw out your partner. Your support system may include friends, family, a trusted counselor, or a wise pastor. Some of these people may show up just when you need them. Others you will have to seek out intentionally. God gifts each person in some way to meet your need, and you can recognize that the love, support, wisdom, feedback, encouragement, and experience that you find in them is God's love overflowing through them to you.

2. *Won by your conduct.* When two people are stalled in an unhealthy pattern of relating to each other, it's not uncommon for one partner to desire change while the other refuses to budge. The one who wants to change begins to feel like a victim to the stubbornness of the other. And then it's so easy to fall into the trap of nagging, pouting, and blaming. Instead of the seesaw ride improving, its imbalance becomes more exaggerated, and no one changes for the better.

The solution is for the partner desiring change to take the initiative. Instead of nagging your spouse, put your energy into loving your spouse. Replace pouting with praying, and blaming with boundaries. This doesn't guarantee that your spouse will choose to change for the better. He or she may decide to walk away, but your odds for winning an irresistible marriage are far better when you choose to learn to do things God's way instead of the old, unhealthy way. And you will gain the priceless treasure of a godly character regardless of what your spouse chooses to do.

Peter talks about winning your unbelieving spouse, not so much by argument but by your godly example.[1] The Bible says that "without a word, [your spouse] may be won by [your] conduct."[2] Wow! What an opportunity awaits us in our own marriages! Truly, actions speak louder than arguments. It was the *love* of Christ that constrained me to follow Him. Likewise, it can be that extravagant love, self-sacrificing love—a "1 Corinthians 13" love—that can, and does, win an unbelieving or uninterested spouse.

An unbalanced zeal

Ruth and Cliff were both nonbelievers until Ruth attended a series of meetings, caught fire, and tried to ignite the same fire in Cliff. Cliff became

---

1. See 1 Peter 3:1, 2.
2. Verse 1.

fired up all right, but not with Ruth's new beliefs. He didn't like change, and he didn't like Ruth's constant Bible thumping about all his wrong ways. He felt that they had had a reasonably good marriage until Ruth's conversion. Now she nagged him continually, but it did no good.

So Ruth recruited help. She asked her new pastor to visit Cliff to try to convert him to "the truth." Cliff quickly discerned the motive behind the well-meaning pastor's visit and dug his heels in even deeper. For twelve years, Ruth and Cliff continued this miserable seesaw—stubbornness on his part and nagging on hers.

I met Ruth and Cliff one day after making a presentation at one of our weekend seminars. How she got him to the meetings, I'll never know. When I saw the two of them, she was practically dragging him by his ear to talk with me. Body language said it all. She expected me to straighten him out, and he felt like a little boy in the principal's office.

Ruth started out enthusiastically. "Jim, I really appreciated your message. That couple you talked about certainly describes us. I'm eager to live the truth, but Cliff, here, just won't get on board. I thought maybe you could talk with him."

I looked at Cliff who was staring at the floor, looking totally miserable.

"Ruth," I began, "I can see that your husband is resistant to talking to me. We can't do anything about him, but we can do a lot about you."

Cliff's ears perked up at that, and I could sense him watching me out of the corner of his eye. I continued, "I sense, Ruth, that you have a heart for doing right and that you want Cliff to get on board with you. But I think you need to put all your efforts into living the truth instead of preaching it. Let Cliff *see* a sermon in shoes instead of being thumped on the head with one."

At that, Cliff came alive and actually exclaimed, "Amen!" Ruth looked at me in disbelief. Her eyes flashed, and her face got red. "Are you saying, Jim, that Cliff doesn't need to change?"

"No, I'm not addressing Cliff right now. I'm addressing you. Quit nagging him and start loving him." I went on to talk with Ruth about the two principles of loving God with our whole being and loving our spouse with nothing in it for ourselves. She began to calm down, and when I finished speaking, she was very quiet. "Thanks, Jim," she said. "I've got a lot to think about."

Cliff, on the other hand, became very animated. Instead of viewing me as the prosecuting attorney, he began to see that he had a friend at court. He asked if he could have some time alone with me. I had time right then, so we went for a walk, and Cliff opened up.

"Jim, I really would like a change in my life. But I haven't seen what I want in Ruth. She has all this new information, but she's not really any different than she used to be. She's the same old Ruth with the same old baggage—except that now she has a self-righteous tongue!"

I don't know what happened with Cliff and Ruth. I never saw them again after that day, but as I have reflected about them since, Romans 1:18 has come to my mind. There are some who hold "the truth in unrighteousness." That was Ruth. She had an extravagant truth, but not an extravagant love. When we combine the two together—truth and love—now, there is a power to convince the unbelieving, ungodly spouse to come on board!

Seriously analyze before God whether you've been trying in your man-managed ways to goad your spouse into changing. If you have, you need to try a new way by allowing God to guide you into extravagant love. So often we attempt to win our spouse by argument when the best argument is a self-denying, self-sacrificing love that will turn our spouse's head and heart.

Turn pouting into praying

When nagging doesn't work, many people begin to pout. My online dictionary defines pouting as showing "disappointment, anger, or resentment, usually in silence."[3] When we pout, we nurse the grievance internally, and it grows in our imagination until it becomes bigger than the reality. Our spouse's good qualities fade to oblivion in our minds, and the distance between us grows. I've never known pouting to help a marriage. Have you?

Instead of pouting, put your energy into intercessory prayer for your partner. God can do big things through prayer. "Prayer is the key in the hand of faith to unlock heaven's storehouse, where are treasured the boundless resources of Omnipotence."[4] Engage with Him—and see what can happen!

My Sally is a big proponent of intercessory prayer. At times in our marriage, she saw things in me that needed to change for the sake of our marriage and home. She would try in her timid way to talk to me about it, but it just wasn't crystal clear in my mind as it was in hers. She decided to resort to intercessory prayer on a daily basis, and she learned what worked and what didn't.

At first, she took her pouting right into her prayers. "Lord, Jim needs to change his temper. He's really insensitive some times, and he makes me feel so bad. I can't take it anymore, Lord. You've just got to do something. Why don't You answer my prayers, Lord?" And she'd rehearse all my shortcomings over and over to the Lord, while her view of me became increasingly

---

3. Encarta® World English Dictionary © 1999 Microsoft Corporation. All rights reserved.

4. Ellen G. White, *Steps to Christ* (Nampa, Idaho: Pacific Press® Publishing Association, 1981), 94.

negative. Later, she told me that she'd get up from praying for me more burdened than when she went to her knees.

As she continued to seek God, He taught her a better way to pray. First, He led her to examine her own heart toward me. "Lord, I confess that I have resentment in my heart toward Jim. I treat him coldly. I ask You to create in me a clean heart toward him and to help me to treat him as You would have me."

Then she would mention the specific weakness that was troubling her. "Lord, hear my prayer. You have joined us together as one. I need Your help. Jim doesn't see where he errs. His temper is out of control at times. [At this point, you can insert your specific issue or issues. It is important in this process to see your spouse as he or she can be in Jesus. This can keep you out of the pit of pouting.]

"Lord," Sally would continue, "Jim has a heart to do the right, but something holds him back. I don't know what that is, but You do. Please help him in the way that You know is best."

The last, but certainly not the least, aspect of intercessory prayer that Sally found was to join hands with God to take whatever action He might lead her to put into place. It might be speaking kind words or opening up a difficult conversation about the issue. It might be showing more loving attentions or taking a stand against evil. It might be crossing my will, making hard decisions, or sharing what she really thought.

"Lord, I'm ready," Sally would pray. "Whatever it takes to turn our marriage around, I'm in it for the long haul. If we need to face financial ruin or a loss of health—whatever hurt, heartache, or pain this will bring—I'm willing. You have my permission to do whatever it will take to change our situation, and I will follow You. Give me Your strength and wisdom to follow the path You will indicate to us."

With this new manner of praying, Sally would get up from her knees feeling lighter. Trust that God would work in our behalf filled her heart, and she'd go about her day with a smile on her face—even though my temper was still unsubdued. It took longer than she wished, but it also happened sooner than she expected. God began to get through to me about my lack of self-control, and I began to change as I recognized my need and surrendered my temper again and again to God. Where Sally's pouting had only added fuel to the fire, her praying made a real change for the better in both of us.

Replace blame with boundaries

Blaming our partner for our troubles is second nature for many of us. Spouses have been playing the blame game ever since that day Adam replied to God, " 'The woman whom You gave to be with me, she gave me of the tree, and I ate.' "⁵ The problem is that blame becomes its own (and only) reward. Blaming puts you in the position of a victim. You feel helpless and run over by your more powerful mate. You feel you don't have much say in the relationship.

Ultimately, blaming replaces loving. One spouse fights off the blame, while the other hunts down him or her. One person gets labeled "the bad guy," while the other is the object of resentment and hurt. Blaming does not solve whatever problems exist. No one wins in the blame game.

A better way than blaming is to honestly confront your mate in love, let him or her know what you will not tolerate, set limits, and, if the behavior continues, give consequences.

This is a touchy subject—especially in our permissive society and churches today. But God sometimes used "lower" motivation to awaken Israel. When nothing else would work, He allowed Israel to be taken captive by the Babylonian armies. Why? Because God loves us so much that if His program of bestowing blessings doesn't move our hearts, He allows the removal of blessings to come into our lives in order to motivate us. "Because the sentence against an evil work is not executed speedily, therefore the heart of the sons of men is fully set in them to do evil."⁶ Not too many like this option in our overly soft Christian climate of the twenty-first century. But it's there in God's Word, and is a legitimate option to be considered in the Lord, not in the flesh.

In my own marriage, Sally was my enabler—at first. She took a very soft, patient, and conciliatory approach with me that strengthened me in my objectionable character traits. Where there are no consequences for ungodly behavior, there is often no motivation to change. If Sally had taken stronger measures to start with, my journey toward a Christlike character might have moved along more rapidly.

How you approach setting limits and giving consequences makes all the difference in the world. Each person is unique and is motivated by different approaches. Be sure you know that your approach and spirit are of God. Then proceed as unto the Lord. You are trying to win your spouse, not whip him or her.

I've known some spouses to say, in the flesh, "I'm not going to cook for you. I'm not going to keep house. I'm going to cut you off. I'll teach you a lesson you will never forget." Well, flesh begets flesh. What you sow you are going to reap. The spirit in which something is delivered makes all the difference between creating more resistance or opening the heart.

---

5. Genesis 3:12.
6. Ecclesiastes 8:11; see also Leviticus 26.

But don't let the fear of addressing an issue in an awkward manner prevent you from addressing it at all. Seek God with a humble heart, ask for His direction, and then move forward. Evaluate with Him all along the way as you experiment with loving limits.

For instance, I have seen men treat their wives with harsh words, a demanding spirit, and sick insensitivity all day long and then expect them to be passionate lovers at night. Impossible! The wife who rewards such behavior becomes her husband's enabler, and they will both reap the results of the loss of true intimacy—for true intimacy comes only as a by-product of two hearts uniting in honesty, affection, and selfless love for the other.

These wives need to communicate honestly to their husbands that if there is no love demonstrated throughout the day, there is no love to be expressed at night. Now, how you go about this, the approach and spirit in which it is accomplished, is vitally important. Don't deliver these thoughts as a punishment. A thousand times, no! Do it to cultivate proper behavior that draws out and nourishes a loving coming together. Improper behavior closes down the heart and emotions and, consequently, the expression of love, as well.

Some well-intentioned Christians interpret the Scriptures that talk about a wife submitting to her husband to mean that she must give up her conscience and yield blind submission to anything and everything her husband wants—regardless of his character, disposition, or desires. They believe the Bible means that the wife should never confront her husband or set loving limits on his behavior.

No! The Scriptures make it clear that God is supreme and that both husband and wife must answer to Him. A wife can yield *total* submission *only* to her Savior who has purchased her with Calvary's blood. Then she can submit to her husband when he is under God. When he is not under God, a wife must remain under God—even if that means crossing her husband.[7]

Boundaries work both ways. When a wife cannot control her spending or can't clean her house on a consistent basis, then the husband, in Christ, needs to stop enabling her. He should lovingly confront her, work on solutions to help her become more responsible, and then allow consequences if real change does not occur.

For instance, he could say in this situation, "Honey, I care about our marriage too much to continue to allow you to run up debt on our credit cards. Until I see that you are able to handle a budget and control your impulsive buying, I will need to remove your credit cards from your use. I know this approach may ruffle some feathers, but I care too much not to do some ruffling."

---

7. See Ephesians 5:22; Colossians 3:18; James 4:7; Acts 5:9.

When confronted, some spouses may argue, "That's just who I am. I was raised that way. You simply have to accept it." But we all could justify our weaknesses with that argument. The gospel is about change. "Because they do not change, Therefore they do not fear God."[8] All of us need to change. Not one of us is perfectly balanced. Extravagant love enters into change with an attitude of wanting to demonstrate our love—not to control our spouse.

The Scriptures say that we should have no fellowship with the unfruitful works of darkness and that God's grace is come to teach us to deny ungodliness and worldly lusts.[9] I believe these texts mean that when our spouse is bent on continuing in habits or practices that are destructive to themselves or others, we must take steps to stop participating in or enabling the destructive behavior and allow our loved one to reap what he or she has sown so that they might want to sow better seed.

The consequences we measure out should be motivated by the attitude that "I love and respect you too much to enable you in a behavior that is destructive to one or both of us and ultimately to our marriage." It is not for me to spell out exactly what you should do in specific situations, but here are some principles to keep in mind when consequences are needed.

- Decide upon action prayerfully and deliberately, not impulsively or out of strong emotion. Take the time to evaluate God's principles and seek to understand your spouse's heart. Pray, pray, pray. Be certain that God, not your flesh, is directing your course of action.
- Consequences should be decision-based—not punishment-focused. What you want to convey is that you love and respect your spouse enough to help him or her to come to a point of decision. You want your spouse to know that you aren't simply venting your frustrations or trying to punish him or her. Making your spouse feel "bad" is not the point.
- Both the consequence itself and the severity of the consequence should be appropriate for the behavior that needs to be changed. For example, if your spouse leaves his dirty clothes on the bathroom floor instead of putting them in the laundry hamper, not washing those clothes with the rest of the laundry would be an appropriate consequence. Withholding emotional closeness would be inappropriately severe and unrelated to the offense.
- The consequence should be enforceable—otherwise it's no better than an empty threat.

---

8. Psalm 55:19.
9. See Titus 2:11, 12; Ephesians 5:11.

- Value your spouse's freedom, as an individual, to make his or her own choices.
- You should respect the rights of your spouse.

3. Unbiased counseling. If you are still deadlocked and stalled, after all your conduct and attempts to reason together, Jesus' principle in Matthew 18:15, 16 calls for bringing outside counsel to bear on the situation. I like this. In fact, many couples need a good facilitator that can help bridge the gap of their dysfunctional reasoning and arguing. You may need to give up your destructive approaches and learn to replace them with constructive approaches that open up communication in a healthy way, rather than closing them down. We are all human, and most of us get in a rut that we just can't seem to get out of without extra help. It's something like needing a tow truck to get your car out of the ditch and back on the road.

If that's the case, ask your spouse whom they would like to use as an outside source of counsel. Don't force this upon them. Approach them with a meek and humble spirit. Make some suggestions without demanding. Perhaps you can find a good professional Christian counselor. Maybe your pastor or a couple you both know and respect would be willing to help you. But find someone you can both agree on and begin the process.

It's best if both parties go into counseling with a listening heart, a spirit that is open to input and solutions. But even if that is not the case, sometimes the objective input of an unbiased counselor can make the difference to help one or both partners see where their attitudes are stalling the relationship.

For instance, Duane and Melanie were stalled over the issue of her chronic lateness. Duane was like me—if you're on time, you're late. If you're early, you're on time. Melanie wasn't at all motivated by the need to be on time. Whenever she got somewhere was soon enough. Duane hated showing up for appointments and meetings late. They argued back and forth about it and got stuck. She thought he was overly conscientious and should lighten up. He was hurt by her unwillingness to budge.

When they started counseling with their pastor, Melanie still held to her opinion that timeliness didn't matter. As the pastor worked with them, he pointed out to Melanie that her attitude toward timeliness was really more about self-centeredness than it was about self-discipline. Suddenly a light went on for Melanie. She saw what her lateness meant to Duane—a lack of love and respect for him as her life partner. Through the perspective of an objective person, she was finally able to see what Duane had been trying to communicate all along, and she began to work on her chronic lateness—not just because Duane was right and she was wrong, but because she truly cared for him.

Counseling was the tow truck that got them out of the ditch and into a practical solution that resolved the problem. Counseling may help you as well. Go back as often as needed until your marriage finds the hope and direction it needs.

4. Long-suffering. Sometimes none of the steps we've listed so far brings about the hoped-for changes. Now you have to decide whether God would have you continue on as you are until your spouse makes a decision or whether to use more extreme measures. I've seen some spouses sit in indecision for years, without receiving any indication from their spouse of a cooperative attitude. Such a situation really tests extravagant love.

In this instant-messaging age, the idea of suffering long—being patient—is not cool. We want resolution now! Immediate results! Let's get on with it! But in God's economy, growth takes time. The sturdiest cedar started from a tiny seed. And that's how people grow too. Change requires the elements of grace, truth, and time.[10]

Grace is accepting your partner with all their good and bad parts and loving them for who they are—not for who you want them to be. It creates a place of safety for your spouse where they can experience compassion and forgiveness. It is essential for growth. Alone, however, it fosters license. It must be exercised in conjunction with truth.

Truth is reality. It is what gives direction and structure to our lives. It supplies the discipline and motivation to identify problems and to seek solutions. Together with grace, truth works to redeem our marriages and us from our stalled condition.

Like sunshine and rain to the sprouting cedar tree, grace and truth must be applied to your marriage, over time, to allow it to grow. Sometimes a lot of growth is taking place under the soil without a lot of evidence on the outside.

For Joe and Joann, resolution took almost sixteen years of Joann demonstrating a long, drawn-out, extravagant love—without any indication of a response on Joe's part. But one day, Joe went to Joann's minister and said, "I want to prepare for baptism. I want what my wife has." By her patient life, Joann turned her husband from the error of his ways, and now both of them are very much enjoying a painless marriage.

I think of Jeff, who for years has patiently endured his wife's liberal lifestyle. In fact, they are in their late sixties. Recently, I received an e-mail from Jeff's wife saying, "Can the three of us meet? I'm ready, and I know Jeff is. We want your help."

---

10. See John 1:14; Luke 13:6–9.

Only God knows what continuous extravagant love will, or will not, produce in your marriage. That's why nobody can tell you how long you need to wait or how many times you should turn your cheek. Only God knows, and it is up to you to connect yourself so closely with Him that He can guide you on your journey. When we marry, we enter into a "covenant love," for better or for worse, in sickness and in health. That is a sacred vow that needs to be lived up to.

Sure, when you married, you expected to experience companionship, intimacy, and oneness with your mate. But even if those hopes have been disappointed, you can have a happy life in a miserable marriage if you work at living out the steps that we discussed in chapters 2 and 3. God is the Fountain of love and joy—and just because your spouse is not cooperating with God's "Plan A" for your marriage doesn't have to mean you are destined to misery. God has promised to supply all your needs, and He will do that for you to the extent that you trust Him and love Him with every fiber of your being.

5. Separation. Yes, separation is a legitimate option when the out-of-control behavior of one spouse jeopardizes the physical, mental, or spiritual health of the other. Even God in heaven had to use separation as a protective hedge against all the spiritual damage Lucifer was causing among the angels.

Separation can be a tool to wake up the offending party and send a serious message that certain situations and behaviors cannot continue. However, don't use separation for the purpose of fleeing your vows or hiding from problems. Separation should help bring your spouse to a life-changing decision while providing an umbrella of protection to the wounded spouse.

Domestic abuse is a huge problem today—both in religious and nonreligious homes. In the year 2001 alone, 588,490 American women were victims of nonfatal violence committed by an intimate partner. On average, more than three women are murdered by their husbands or boyfriends in the United States every day.[11] And although the vast majority of victims of domestic violence are women, men can also be the targets of abuse.

Domestic abuse includes more than physical violence. It can include emotional abuse, sexual abuse, economic abuse, and isolation. Domestic abuse occurs when one spouse tries to dominate and control the other person. He or she uses fear, guilt, shame, and intimidation to wear down the other and gain complete power over him or her. The abusive spouse may threaten his or her partner or hurt that person or others in the family. The

---

11. Bureau of Justice Statistics, Crime Data Brief, Intimate Partner Violence, 1993–2001, February 2003.

abusive spouse does not recognize the personhood of his or her partner and treats the spouse as an enemy who must be conquered rather than as a partner who should be loved and valued.

Such abusive situations are an entirely different issue than two equal partners airing out differing opinions and working to find solutions. Abusive situations are rarely resolved without separation. Continuing to live with abuse leaves long-term scars for you, your children, and the abuser. Separating could be one of the most loving things you could do.

If you are the victim of abuse, seek help from God and from those in your community who can support you and help you make a plan and take effective action.

Often after separation occurs, abusers will have "a spiritual experience" and promise that they will never abuse their partner again. Affirm this decision and attitude, but remain suspicious. If an abuser is truly willing to change and reconcile with you, he or she will do the hard work of entering into spiritual counseling, therapeutic counseling, and group therapy.

In cases of abuse, marriage counseling shouldn't be considered until all parties feel that the abuser is making progress with his or her character issues. Evaluate his dedication to supporting his family. Is he paying child and spousal support? Is she faithful in seeking Christian fellowship? Does she obey all court orders? Does he consistently attend therapy sessions? Until the abuser shows progress in working on the abuse issue, no other marital problems can be solved. Abuse is a cloud that obscures all other behaviors and communication problems. As long as abuse is an issue, the victim can't realistically be expected to face any other marital issues, even those in which he or she needs to make changes.

Marital separation is not an easy road. But if God leads you in that path, you can walk safely with Him, and you can be sure that He is working on your behalf—and on behalf of your abusive spouse—to create irresistible love. At times, it may seem impossible, but all things are possible with God! Don't lose heart. God is there for you!

A note about divorce

God prescribed a very narrow escape clause from the marriage contract: " 'Except for sexual immorality.' "[12] Why is that? Why does our culture—and even the church—seem to look for ways to stretch this stipulation? Why did God so strictly limit His allowance for the dissolution of a marriage?

I believe it is because marriage represents the truth of covenant love in which God wants all of us to find our security. When that covenant is vio-

---

12. Matthew 19:9.

lated, the security of husbands, wives, children, relatives, community, and society is shaken. That's why God hates divorce.[13] It cuts right at the heart of everything that home and family are meant to be. Consequently, He calls all of us to live within an attitude of enduring commitment and to grow in a spirit of forgiveness and reconciliation.

Divorce doesn't solve a problem marriage; it ends it. God permits divorce in extreme cases, but does not command it. God would much rather heal the marriage. We need to fight for our marriages. They are worth the effort! I have known couples to be married for thirty years, both spouses become involved in adultery, and still turn their affections back to one another.

Too many people I've counseled with believe that their marriage problems are the result of marrying the wrong person. They think that if only they could have a different partner, things would be different. Often, both spouses have baggage within themselves that they haven't dealt with, because they were too caught up in nagging, pouting, or blaming their spouse. They think the next marriage partner will be better suited to them, only to find—in time—that the new spouse has even worse baggage then did their former spouse and that they still haven't dealt with their own internal, unresolved issues. If you haven't dealt with your own character issues in one marriage, they will continue to cause problems in the next. Just changing partners is not the solution.

And yet, if divorce becomes the best option for your situation, don't lose heart. With Christ as your Companion, you can build a home of peace and security—even if it is in singleness.

Take heart!

I can't overemphasize the importance in this whole process of actively, wholeheartedly, and untiringly applying the first principle discussed in this chapter. None of us are sufficient of ourselves to remedy a broken or hurting marriage. Only God can read your heart and the heart of your spouse. Only He knows the length of time needed, the motivations necessary, and the sacrifice required to make your marriage irresistible.

Never give up until you are sure God is asking you to let it go. What may look impossible to your human eyes may be very possible in the eyes of infinite Love. Just a little over a year ago, my personal assistant was separated from her husband. Both she and I would have given her marriage about a 5 percent chance of surviving. But today, her marriage is fantastic! With God, she and her husband took their marriage from incompatible to irresistible! And, with God, you and your spouse can too!

---

13. See Malachi 2:16.

Study Questions for Chapter 8

1. Are you willing to take whatever steps necessary to turn the heart of your spouse from the error of his or her ways?
2. Does the conduct of your life match the words of your profession?
3. Are you willing to let your little light shine in order to awaken a glow in your spouse?
4. Are you open to nonbiased marriage counseling?
5. Do you believe "additional motivations" can be used effectively if done "in the Lord"?
6. Are you willing to continue in your "covenant love" until it turns into "extravagant love" on both sides?
7. Due to drastic circumstances, is God calling you to separate from your spouse in order to motivate a decision and/or to protect the innocent parties?
8. Why do you think "God hates divorce"?

CHAPTER 9

From Incompatible to Irresistible

*"I will bring the blind by a way they did not know;
I will lead them in paths they have not known.
I will make darkness light before them,
And crooked places straight.
These things I will do for them,
And not forsake them."*

—Isaiah 42:16

It was Sabbath morning. Jeanette was up early, putting the final touches on her program for the children's Sabbath School, getting piano music ready for church, preparing food for potluck, and making breakfast. Her eight-year-old son, Bradley, was in the shower, and Rady, her husband, was still in bed. Thinking of Rady triggered conflicting emotions regarding the unresolved conflict of the day before—which, in reality, was just another layer of smoldering tension added to years of misunderstanding and hurt. Jeanette couldn't tell which emotion was the stronger—a longing for the lost sweetness of their brief courtship or resentment over the bitterness of their present reality.

Tears came to her eyes as she thought about "Fond Lane." She and Rady hadn't known each other very long when he had invited her to walk down the lane in front of her parents' home. It had been one of those romantic moonlit nights, and Rady posed the question on his heart. "Jeanette, I've grown rather fond of you, and I wondered if there could ever be more than friendship between us."

Blushing, Jeanette caught her breath. After a bit of surprised hesitation, she murmured, "I'm growing fond of you too." Their moonlight walk ended with a warm embrace that ignited a whirlwind courtship.

They found themselves irresistibly in love and talking for hours on end. They found that there was no subject they couldn't share. Their mutual transparency quickly knit their hearts together. Rady was warm, empathetic, and understanding. He treated Jeanette like a princess and made her feel that, in his eyes, she could do no wrong. Jeanette was soft-spoken, thoughtful, and personable. She kept herself physically fit and enjoyed the same strenuous outdoor activities—running and rock climbing—that Rady did.

I've often said that "spark" is one of the essential ingredients needed (among others)[1] by couples contemplating marriage. Well, Rady and Jeanette had spark! You could feel it radiating from across the room. Their attraction for each other was tangible, powerful, sweet, and irresistible.

It was blissful, wonderful. They each felt that they had found the love of their lives and could hardly wait to get married. Both Rady and Jeanette had experienced the failure and loss of previous marriages, and each longed for a more fulfilling relationship. They resolved that they would continue to communicate after getting married and that they would not allow a day to go by without resolving hurt feelings or misunderstandings.

Irresistible to incompatible

How could their good intentions, solemn promises, and fervent desires have slipped away so quickly? Instead of the bliss they had expected, they found themselves riding a seesaw they had never identified or dealt with in their previous relationships. Rady became demanding, irritable, and selfish at home—while continuing to be a model elder at church. Jeanette did her best to outwardly comply with Rady's demands, but inwardly she felt victimized and struggled with bitter resentment that erupted in angry words and gestures from time to time.

Yesterday had been no different. As Jeanette thought about it, resentment rose up in her heart like a tidal wave poised to crush out any tender feelings she had been experiencing.

Rady and Jeanette had heard the call for country living and were building a cute little home in rural Idaho. To save money, they were living in the house while they finished it one room at a time. The day before this particular Sabbath, they had been painting a bedroom. Jeanette was using a brush in the corners, while Rady used a roller to cover the main areas. Jeanette was doing her best to be helpful, but she just couldn't seem to get it right.

Rady glanced over his shoulder, sighed in irritation, and blurted out, "Come on, Jeanette, can't you see you're painting with a dry brush? How many times do I have to tell you not to use a dry brush? Do you need to get your eyes checked?"

Jeanette's eyes flashed indignation, but she bit her tongue and put more paint on her brush. A few moments later, Rady looked over again and snorted his disgust. "Now you're putting way too much paint on! Can't you see it's going to run?"

---

1. See the bonus chapter for guidelines for couples considering whether they are meant for each other.

Angrily grabbing the brush out of her hand, he pushed her aside. "I guess I'll have to do it all myself. I don't know what's so hard about it." Giving her one more glare, he ordered, "Why don't you go make lunch? I'll eat after I finish doing *your* corners."

Fuming, Jeanette stomped out of the room, down the stairs, and into the kitchen. Rady continued painting, frustrated at Jeanette's ineptness. Soon he finished the task and went downstairs to eat.

"Is lunch ready yet?" he demanded.

"Not quite," she snapped defensively.

"Dollar waiting on a dime," he commented sarcastically.

Oh, how Jeanette hated that statement! It seemed to be one of Rady's favorite ways to rub it in that his needs, his wishes, his projects, his time, his priorities were more important than hers. At least, that's how it felt to her. Again, Jeanette bit her tongue. But her anger expressed itself very loudly through her body language as she stomped back and forth setting the table.

Jeanette called Bradley to the table, but Rady had already said his own prayer and was eating. She and Bradley prayed and then ate in silence. When Rady finished eating, he left the table and flopped down on the couch for a nap, while Jeanette and Bradley washed the dishes.

Now, on Sabbath morning, these scenes and others like them replayed themselves over and over again in Jeanette's mind. *Why can't Rady be nice? Why can't he see past his own nose once in a while?* The resentment rose up, but she stuffed it down. After all, Christians don't get angry.

Meanwhile, upstairs in bed, Rady reflected on the week. He had a vague sense that all was not well in their marriage—and to be honest, he wasn't happy either—but he shrugged it off. To him, this was normal family life. He didn't like it when Jeanette was miffed, but he figured there was nothing he could do about it.

The family rode to church in silence, each absorbed in their own thoughts. When they arrived, Rady became a different person. He smiled, visited pleasantly, shook hands with everyone, hugged a few, and led out as platform elder with enthusiasm.

Jeanette was used to this transformation, but she always wondered, *Why can't he be like that at home? Why can't he treat me at least as well as he does the people at church?* It was the same at the grocery store, the bank, or wherever Rady worked. She decided it would be nicer *not* to be his wife. Then they'd be better friends. But it was too late now. Stuffing down her resentment once more, Jeanette pasted on a smile and went about her church duties.

Can you relate to Rady and Jeanette? Have you and your spouse ever played the game of being one thing in private and another in public? Rady and Jeanette were zealous about many good things. They threw themselves into country living, health reform, dress reform, and homeschooling. They were active with church duties and outreach to the community. They even took a three-week mission trip to India, held evangelistic meetings, and helped start a new church. All of these things were good in their proper place, but they could not substitute for addressing the issues that were making their home unhappy.

Rady and Jeanette continued to ride this miserable seesaw for a number of years until one day Jeanette made an unwelcome announcement, "Honey, I'm pregnant." She carefully watched Rady's face hoping for a tender response.

But all Rady could think of was the added responsibility a baby would mean. He already felt overwhelmed, and the thought of yet another "problem" on his plate was more than he could bear. His face reddened, and the muscles in his neck tightened as he blurted out in frustration, "Well why did you let *that* happen? Maybe we'll be lucky and you'll have another miscarriage!"

The words stabbed like a dagger. Jeanette wanted that baby! But after three months, Rady got his wish. Jeanette tried to absorb the loss, but found herself mired in grief and depression that she could not throw off. Her depression hindered her ability to cater to Rady's demands. He responded with more criticism, which only deepened her depression. Their seesaw ride was caught in a downward spiral.

"Just as I am"

Jeanette craved a stable sense of love and acceptance, but she could see that Rady was not going to provide what she needed. In desperation, she began to reach out to God in a way she never had before. Without realizing it, she was applying principle one that we discussed early in this book: turning from broken cisterns and going to the Fountain. Instead of merely going through the motions of reading her Bible, praying, and performing her church duties, Jeanette began to let God into her pain and struggles. She clung to Jesus' promise in John 6:37 like a drowning victim grabs on to a lifesaver—" 'the one who comes to Me I will by no means cast out.' "

Heartbroken, and at the end of her resources, she cried, "Lord, I'm tired of playing the game of religion on the outside while I'm miserable and wretched on the inside. If You are real, then what You have to offer has to work for *me* where the rubber meets *my* road. I'm coming to You just as I am. I'm like one of those 'whited sepulchers' You talked about—looking good at playing the game of religion, while on the inside I'm riddled with rotten emotions, tortured thoughts, and unresolved pain. I see that I can't save myself or fix myself. I just cast myself upon Your mercy."

She quit trying to rise above her crushing burdens, and as she did so, she found herself in the arms of God. He was there just waiting for this moment. Instead of condemning her for her brokenness, He wrapped her in His arms and whispered tenderly in her ear, " 'Fear not, for I have redeemed you; I have called you by your name; You are Mine.' "[2]

Oh, the relief, the blessedness of being released from the struggle and resting in the arms of God! He truly was to Jeanette a gushing Fountain of life, and she clung to Him, drinking deeply to quench her thirst. She found herself breathing Psalm 139 as a constant prayer: "O Lord, You have searched me and known me [and still loved me]. . . . Lead me in the way everlasting."[3]

God began to lead her into a process of examining her deepest beliefs about Him and life—and therein she discovered the root of her misery. Without realizing it, Jeanette had allowed *people* to occupy the place in her heart that belongs only to God.

Jeanette was a people-pleaser, afraid to think for herself, feeling bound by the expectations of strong people around her, especially her husband. She lived for the approval of others and never felt she measured up. She resented the control Rady had over her, but thought that it was her duty to be pleasing and compliant. She felt she had no choice—that God, too, expected this of her. Her problem-solving technique when faced with conflict was to have no opinions or thoughts of her own, to be as passive and small as possible, and to let the other person rule. If she didn't please others, she feared abandonment and rejection. But when she did manage to please, the approval she received was short-lived, and her disappointment expressed itself as anger, resentment, jealousy, and envy.

God began to teach Jeanette that what another person wants or expects does not necessarily mean that God expects this of her. God wanted to have an individual experience with Jeanette and direct her personally. He wanted to help her develop her individuality so that she could say "No" when she needed to, express her own thoughts and opinions, and hold her own in a relationship.

---

2. Isaiah 43:1.
3. Verses 1, 24.

Happy in a miserable marriage

"Do You mean, Lord," she asked, "that I can be a happy wife in a miserable marriage? That I can be content even if Rady treats me poorly?"

"Yes! Rady is not the one who supplies all your needs—I am. My 'Plan A' is to work through Rady to meet your needs, but if he fails to do that, My hand is not tied. I can still fill you with love, joy, and peace—regardless of your circumstances."

As Jeanette entered into this experience with God, she began to taste a freedom she had never known before. She had found a solid Rock to build on, and she would never be the same again.

As principle one began to find an ongoing practical application in her life, principle two became meaningful. Instead of desperately trying to please Rady so that he would prop her up with his approval, she began to follow God's lead in relating to Rady. She began to learn how to love her husband deeply without her own self-interest being the principle motive.

For example, God asked Jeanette to start greeting Rady at the door with a warm hug, a kiss, and a smile when he came home from work—even when Rady was treating her coldly and she didn't feel like doing it. It took every ounce of surrender and trust in God, but when she followed His leading, she found a freedom she had never experienced before.

At times, God led her to say "No" to Rady's expectations, which challenged the weakest part of her personality. She was so used to caving in. She would wrestle inwardly and find in God the strength to stand up to Rady's displeasure. When Rady gave her the cold shoulder while treating others warmly, Jeanette learned to find contentment in God instead of withdrawing resentfully. She began to study and practice how to be a better wife, homemaker, and mother; she learned how to make emotional connections on a deeper level, rather than staying superficial. She became much more stable emotionally. Don't think this was easy for her. It was not—because Rady's response was not what you might expect!

Rady saw the change in Jeanette, but instead of being pleased, he was alarmed. She was becoming happy and content. Rady's history had taught him to seek for control rather than connection. Now his previous sense of control was vanishing, and in its place he began to feel the distance between himself and Jeanette that had been there all along. He could no longer "push her buttons" and get the same response.

Rady's negative response to Jeanette's freedom challenged her to the core. She wrestled over and over again with the dilemma: Would she hold on to her freedom and keep growing in God? Or would she cower and return to the old ways?

Jeanette chose to take steps forward in her newfound Christian experience. Over and over, she affirmed, "I believe that God can change me. I believe that God can change Rady. And I believe that, with God, we can have a happy home." She was sure that, in time, Rady would want what she was finding and that then home would become happier.

Instead, the tension seemed to mount. She didn't understand it! She was becoming a better homemaker, more cheerful, helpful, and thoughtful—but Rady seemed to become more and more morose and overbearing.

She tried to understand, but all her attempts to reach out to her husband were met with a cold shoulder or bitter rebuffs. The more time passed, the greater became the tension. Rady was stuck in some misbeliefs that he needed to face, but he feared change so deeply that he would not "go there," and so the misbeliefs were not identified and replaced with truth. This tug-of-war intensified over a period of six years.

During this time, Rady, Jeanette, and Bradley attended our Empowered Living camp meetings. We observed a quiet, good-looking family who presented themselves well. Sally worked with Jeanette on some parenting issues, and Jeanette started to correspond with Sally about her spiritual journey. Little by little, we began to piece together what was happening behind closed doors.

Rady and I sat on a park bench together at one camp meeting and talked at length about the Christian experience and how that should translate into our closest relationships. Rady was very good at discussing the theory, but when I directed the conversation toward practical application, Rady became very vague and refused to make a commitment. Rady is not alone in this. I meet a lot of men—and some women too—like Rady. They keep the truth in the outer court. When I try to help them take it to the inner court with simple decisions, such as committing to say one affirming thing to their spouse every day, they won't go there. They avoid it, stall, and put it off.

The tension between Rady and Jeanette continued to increase. The stress was becoming debilitating. Jeanette had learned to be a happy wife in a miserable marriage, yet the lack of a resolution to the issues the family faced took its toll on her health and energy. She was deeply committed both to her husband and to God, but if God and her husband were not in agreement, she would follow God.

Five options

God began to show Jeanette that extravagant love is not content with the status quo. It seeks redemptive change. While respecting the rights of the other, it will not participate in evil. As the stalemate in their home increased,

Jeanette prayed and studied and tried every approach she could think of to make peace without compromising her conscience.

She called us one day and shared her struggle. I suggested that she had five options similar to those we discussed in the previous chapter.

1. *Keep doing what you're doing.* Jeanette was already under conviction that God was calling her to do something different. The situation was destructive to all three of them in their family.

2. *Divorce.* This is an option many take. If they've beaten their heads against a brick wall for six years, they consider that they've done enough and bail out. But Jeanette and Rady didn't have biblical grounds for a divorce. Furthermore, Jeanette didn't want divorce. She wanted to see their marriage mended. Rather than become another sad statistic, she wanted it to become a memorial of God's mercy.

3. *Counseling.* They could both apply godly counsel and fix their marriage. That is what Jeanette wanted, but she didn't know if Rady would agree to it.

4. *Consequences.* If Rady would not agree to counseling or to follow through on the counsel, she would need to allow him to experience the consequences of his choices—not to punish him, but to limit the destructive effects of his behavior on her and to encourage a decision in a positive direction.

5. *Separate.* If counseling and consequences did not resolve the tension, they would have to choose between continuing to live with it or to separate.

Jeanette wrestled for weeks. She was reluctant to present these options to Rady because she knew he would feel backed into a corner, and she didn't want to do that to him. She also feared he would decide she wasn't worth fighting for and would abandon her.

Rady sensed that Jeanette was thinking through things and feared he was losing her and everything he held dear. But he was stuck in inaction until one morning when he bolstered his courage and confronted Jeanette. "I just want to know what you are planning to do."

That's when she told him about the five options. Just as Jeanette feared, Rady felt like she was handing down an ultimatum and that he didn't have a choice. He began to cry and told Jeanette that he didn't want to lose her or Bradley.

Rady's tears gave Jeanette hope. His behavior had told her that he hated her. His tears told her that he still wanted to make their marriage work. Rady chose the option of counseling and wanted to counsel with Sally and me. Jeanette and Rady knelt to pray with tears flowing freely. They committed to God that they would do whatever it might take to repair their marriage so that it would honor Him. It seemed that they had reached a turning point.

They didn't know it then, but the greatest struggles were still ahead. It's one thing to agree to the truth—but implementing it in your life can feel like cutting off your arm or gouging out your eye.

I'll never forget those counseling sessions with Jeanette and Rady—although they are not unlike many couples we've worked with. On one side, is a spouse who is willing and anxious to get on with repairing the marriage. They are excited. They're finally going to find some solutions! They interact, admit their part of the problem, and engage in the solution.

With the other spouse, you feel more like a dentist than a friend. They don't hear you. They don't get it. They're silent and resistant. They act like you're leading them into a field of land mines. They respond with a lot of "uhs," "yeahs," and " 'sposes."

Rady had heard us talk about removing thorns from a marriage, so he came ready with his list of "thorns" that Jeanette needed to remove. But I felt impressed to take a different direction with them. You see, if you can restore love in a relationship, the thorns are easily removed. So I gave them the assignment of doing what made each other feel loved—and not doing what made each other feel unloved. I asked each of them to write down three things that they wanted the other to do and three things they would like the other to stop doing—and then exchange lists. I asked them to follow those lists every day.

Jeanette responded with enthusiasm; Rady was silent. He told us later that he felt a huge wave of resistance come over him. He was longing for a deep connection of love and had been trying to get it by stonewalling, demanding, and controlling. That approach wasn't working, and yet he found it overwhelmingly threatening to give it up.

After what felt like a lot of "teeth pulling," Rady agreed to try. But after a couple of days, he gave it up. So the next week, we tried to talk the situation through and then took a different approach. This continued for several months. We couldn't seem to get things off the ground. Rady would step out with good intentions, but quickly return to the old pattern.

Meanwhile, Jeanette was struggling with hopelessness. She didn't like the direction things were taking. She only wanted to be on the same page with both God and Rady and to have a happy home. She didn't want to give consequences—that seemed like a parental role. She did a lot of praying and heart searching and concluded that she loved and respected Rady—the real Rady hidden away inside—too much to continue enabling their dysfunction.

"I can't choose for him, but I can choose for me," she told herself.

She decided to let Rady know that unless he demonstrated over the following two weeks a real willingness to apply the counsel and make changes, she would ask him to move to the guest bedroom—knowing what a low blow that would be to him.

Rady sensed further alienation and rejection—which seemed to incapacitate him for making changes. He moved to the guest bedroom without a fight, but over the next few months, he soured even more. The stalemate was increasing—not decreasing.

About that time, Empowered Living Ministries purchased property and drew up plans for a ministry office. We started looking for a builder and found that the ones in our area were already booked up. As I prayed about it one day, Rady came to my mind. I knew he was a builder—but would he be available? And would he be interested in building for us?

To make a long story short, he was available and willing! By the beginning of June 2005, the Houghtelling family was in Montana living in a small fifth-wheel trailer on the building site.

Now keep in mind that Rady and Jeanette had been sleeping in separate bedrooms for over four months. But trailers don't have guest bedrooms! With the limited space, Rady felt like things were back to "normal"—and indeed, this building project provided a six-month respite with many opportunities to make changes. But, sadly, no positive changes were made. From my perspective, Rady became more sullen, sour, and stubborn; anyone who spent time with Jeanette and Rady could sense the mounting tension.

Breaking the stalemate

Jeanette knew she had only one more option, but she didn't want to face it. She feared that separation would mean the end—failure, total ruin, unredeemable alienation. She wanted to fix their marriage, not end it! And yet her only options were to live with unending, irresolvable, escalating tension or to separate.

She struggled, prayed, wept, studied, and counseled for several months, and the conviction grew that she needed to break the stalemate by initiating a separation. But she kept stalling. She didn't want to do it. To her, separation felt like committing emotional and social suicide.

She finally put out a fleece—a test—in which she asked God to make His direction clear to her. The answer that came back was not what she wanted: separation. Finally, she agreed with God to take the step.

When Rady received Jeanette's letter asking for a separation, he was first shocked and devastated, and then angry. He tried to intimidate Jeanette, to bargain with her. But her mind was made up. She believed that God had asked her to close the door on living in a tension-filled home. The peace of God would rule in her home. If Rady would make the changes he needed to make to be a part of that, she would be delighted. If not, she was willing to face the rest of her life as a single person.

When the reality of the separation finally sank in, Rady felt overwhelmed and paralyzed by a sense of total emptiness. His worst fears had become reality. He began looking in earnest for real love by deep heart searching and weeping—crying out to God, day after day, to break through his miserable existence.

God answered his prayer through a Depression Recovery series at his local church. There Rady found helpful information, supportive people who wanted to grow, and a new concept that transformed his life: identifying one's own self-talk. What you tell yourself, you believe, and it becomes the rule in your life. Rady began to realize that he—not Jeanette—had been his own worst enemy and that God would help him to resolve the inner struggle that had been his reality all of his life. He grasped the fact that God had not abandoned him and that He would be with him in his struggle.

Rady began to tell himself the truth:

- "I may feel lonely, but I am not alone."
- "With God, I can face my fear of 'going there' and begin to explore why I do what I do."
- "My fear of not being understood doesn't have to stop me from trying to explain myself."
- "I may feel unacceptable, but God says that He accepts me, and I will believe Him over my feelings and history."
- "I can own my anger instead of stuffing it inside. With God, I can explore issues and change the negativity in my thoughts and feelings."
- "I don't have to give up so easily. Other people have gotten through these kinds of situations and turned their lives around. With God's help, I can too."

Little by little, Rady began to feel a sense of well-being replacing his misery. He was applying the first of the two principles—returning to the Fountain of living waters—and it was beginning to work.

During this process, he would see Jeanette from time to time—usually on Sundays. They went out to eat, cross-country skied, or worked on projects on the property they owned together. Jeanette watched their interaction closely to see if real change was occurring in Rady's approach to her. Time after time, her hopes would be raised, only to be disappointed again. Rady was growing in personal freedom, but didn't yet understand how to translate that into his relationship with Jeanette.

By this time, Jeanette's emotions were raw. The prolonged struggle, together with her strong feelings of failure and embarrassment, overwhelmed her, and her health broke. She experienced intense feelings of shame that were written all over her countenance. She felt extremely isolated—even from God. She knew she had taken this step with Him, and yet she often could not sense His presence with her. She felt all alone.

When Rady became involved at church, it felt very much like the old program to Jeanette. Women would call her or come up to her and say, "Your husband is such a wonderful man!" That felt like the final insult—twisting appearances to make her look like an unreasonable and ungrateful woman. Her health was low, and the sense of isolation, disapproval, and lack of understanding made her feel locked into a situation in which she was too weak to stand up for herself.

Breakthrough!

Rady was asking for more time with Jeanette, but she started spending *less* time with him. She felt a need to let her raw emotions heal. About this time, someone gave Rady the book *Discovering the Mind of a Woman* by Ken Nair, and encouraged him to read it. The person offering him the book didn't know that Rady had actually started to read it three years earlier—only to put it down after a while, saying, "This is not for me!"

This time, however, Rady read it. Not only that, but he was fully motivated to take in its counsel and apply it in his life. More than anything else, Rady wanted to repair the damage he had done to his marriage and see it turn around. As he read the book, the concept of accountability and the responsibility of the man in the marriage became very apparent to him; it spoke to his heart at the core. The dysfunction that he had cultivated for so long in his mind began to unravel.

It finally dawned on Rady that Jeanette has a spirit and that God was requiring him—as her husband—to care for her spirit. God started teaching Rady about investing in relationships—something that was very foreign to him, because he was so used to thinking only of his own needs.

Rady began to see that the issue was character and that God was holding him accountable. He saw that God wanted his heart and wanted to restore him to His image. Rady determined to seek to become Christlike, even if he and Jeanette never got back together. In other words, his motivation changed. He was no longer doing it for Jeanette—he was investing in himself to become the new creature, the new man that he had been avoiding for so long. It was between God and him alone. He was able to put away his defensiveness and change his approach to relationships. He began to be more aware of how he affected others, to focus more on what he could give, rather than on what he could get, and to be consciously aware of what motivated him.

He helped start a men's study group to discuss these concepts one evening a week. He told Jeanette what he was doing and was surprised at her response. As she told me, "Rady is going to prove to everyone—except me—that he knows how to treat a woman. What phony baloney!" Deep down inside, though, she wished with all her heart that the change in Rady could really work. More than anything in the world, she wanted it to be true—but she couldn't handle being deceived again and pretending that things were OK when they weren't.

I wondered if Jeanette's response would discourage Rady. But it didn't. He realized that he was in it for the long haul, because long-term damage had occurred to their marriage and that he had been at the center of inflicting the damage, even though he hadn't recognized it. He hung in there because he believed that God was restoring him and that God could restore their marriage.

By this time, Rady and Jeanette had been separated for a year and nine months. Jeanette was beginning to think that their marriage was over and was settling in to live the rest of her life as a single person. She gave their marriage about a 5 percent chance of coming around.

By this time, Rady was beginning to find a freedom he had never felt before and couldn't wait to share it with Jeanette. Yet he felt the walls of Jericho between them. He prayed for continued change on his part and that it would be transparent to Jeanette during the few times they interacted.

For some time, it didn't look like it was going anywhere, and then Rady decided to muster up all his courage to invite Jeanette on a picnic.

She thought to herself, *Here we go again, another waste of time.* But out loud she replied, "Let me pray about it, and I'll get back to you." As she prayed about it, she felt strongly impressed to accept. When she told him—and offered to bring the food—he was shocked but began to put his plans into action.

He had found a really special out-of-the-way place that he knew Jeanette would like—a place where a small creek came meandering out of the forest and cascaded down a double falls into a canyon below. The two of them met after church and slipped away by themselves to this special spot.

It was a warm, sunny day, and Rady felt that he was breaking through some ice. After they ate and chatted about this and that, Rady began to share some of the things he was understanding about himself and how he had come to understand the way his actions had affected their home. He asked for her thoughts and feedback.

Jeanette could hardly believe her ears. Rady was looking her in the eye with a sincerity and earnestness she hadn't seen before. He appeared to actually listen to what she had to say—listening for her heart, not just arguing with her words. He encouraged her to say more. He freely admitted his share of the responsibility in the breakdown of their home and seemed genuinely sorry for the hurt he had caused. The brick wall she was so used to hitting was gone! She started sharing just a bit more—testing the waters—and he didn't get mad or shut down.

When they went home that night, Jeanette couldn't help it. Her hopes were soaring, and she didn't want them to. She was sure it wouldn't last—and yet she couldn't deny how their hearts had connected at a deeper level than she had ever experienced through sixteen years of marriage. She found it irresistible!

Rady went home that night higher than a kite! He realized that what had happened was the result of cooperating with God (principle one) and of implementing his new discoveries in how to treat a woman the way she needs to be treated—becoming sensitive to her spirit and taking the initiative to care for it (principle two).

That picnic marked the beginning of Rady's and Jeanette's second courtship. God was giving them a chance to do it over right. They began to spend Sabbaths together—sitting together in church, hiking, reading, and talking—heart-to-heart talking. On Sundays, they cut firewood together, did yard work together, went backpacking, and spent a lot of time talking. Over the next few months, the changes lasted and deepened. Rady was real—the real man was coming out. At last, the two of them were on the same page—both loving God supremely and caring for each other unselfishly.

January 1, 2008, after twenty-five months of separation (and nine-and-a-half years after Jeanette took that first step with God), Rady and Jeanette reunited their home—and what a different home it is now! It is peaceful, pleasant, and happy. Sure, each of them still have weaknesses to overcome, and they face bumps in the road from time to time, but they're now both headed in the same direction. They are both engaged with applying the two principles of chapters 2 and 3 on a continual basis—and it works! They have become irresistible again!

Study Questions for Chapter 9

1. Do you believe that, with God, you can have a happy home?
2. Do you believe that God can change you—with your cooperation?
3. Do you believe that He can change your spouse—with their cooperation?
4. What could God do for your marriage and home if one or both of you implemented principles one and two as discussed earlier in this book?
5. Will you start where you are and say, "It begins with me," even if your spouse is not on board?
6. Where is God asking you to begin today?

CHAPTER 10

Pass It On!

*"And they overcame Him by the blood of the Lamb
and by the word of their testimony,
and they did not love their lives to the death."*
—*Revelation 12:11*

J. D. and Alecia were on cloud nine! Instead of having their bubble burst, it was more filled than ever. They had seemed a bit nervous and timid when they first arrived, but now they were free and jubilant. They just *knew* that their marriage was going to be the exception to the sad statistics—and now they had practical tools to make it so!

That memorable afternoon was coming to a close. They had asked wonderful questions—insightful questions. And their interaction told me they were taking in what I shared with them. I was thrilled!

I wanted to leave them with one more thing—a sense of mission, a vision that would give focus to their lives. I wanted to inspire them with God's purpose to use them to draw others to Himself through the living testimony of their lives.

I looked into those glowing young faces and said, "Remember that you've got to continually apply these principles—and when you do, you will have an irresistible marriage. Then pass it on! Our world is crying out for a practical demonstration of the power of God in our marriages and homes. The two of you can do nothing more powerful in making a positive difference in the world around you than to build an irresistible marriage. The family is the building block of society, and marriage is its foundation. That foundation is crumbling—with devastating effects on our children and society at large.

"It's a tragic reality that over a million American children experience the divorce of their parents each year. And half of the children born this year to parents who are married will see their parents divorce before they turn eighteen. Mounting evidence demonstrates that divorce has devastating physical, emotional, and financial effects on children that last well into adulthood and negatively affects future generations.[1] When parents place a low priority on building an irresistible marriage, they contribute to the downward spiral of society.

"But that doesn't have to be you, Alecia and J. D.! By God's grace, you can pass on a different kind of legacy to your children—the legacy of an irresistibly happy marriage! Children who live in homes filled with warmth, free-flowing communication, and physical and emotional safety, develop a secure emotional base that can go with them for life. In turn, they will be more likely to have happy marriages and perpetuate a positive influence to the next generation.

"So build an irresistible marriage. Make God the Center and Guide of your lives. Stick with each other through the lows of life as well as its highs. Then pass it on! Pass it on to your children! Pass it on to your neighbors, to your fellow Christians, and as God opens the way, pass it on to the world! You can make a difference!"

As I saw J. D. and Alecia to the door, I could sense a new air of confidence about them—as well as the tingles they had arrived with. Their heads, their hearts, and their wills were fully engaged. Hand in hand, they walked through the gently falling snowflakes and drove off with an even deeper commitment to each other and to their marriage.

What will the rest of their story be?

I didn't see J. D. and Alecia again until their wedding day. As I sat in the audience watching those two pledge their love to each other, I couldn't help wondering what the final story would be for them. Sally and I have counseled so many couples. Those that have applied the two principles I outlined to J. D. and Alecia have seen their marriages empowered and revitalized. Those who didn't engage or who tired of the effort remained stuck in mediocrity or went their separate ways. Which would it be for this young couple?

My thoughts turned to my own marriage. Where would Sally and I be today if fame and fortune had remained center stage in our lives? Where would my boys be today had we not made our marriage a top priority? I shuddered to contemplate it. I have no regrets for doing what it took to connect with God and bring our hearts together. The joy we experience has filled us with a passion to help others find what we are finding.

God calls us not just to live to ourselves. We are to pour ourselves out for the benefit of humanity. Our responsibility is not just to teach people about the Bible. It is our responsibility to teach them who God is through a living

---

1. Patrick F. Fagan and Robert Rector, *The Effects of Divorce on America,* Heritage Foundation Backgrounder, no. 1373, June 5, 2000.

experience. They need to see Him in our eyes, read Him on our faces, hear Him in our voices, and witness Him in our interactions with our spouses.

We are to leave out no one. Not the communists or Muslims. Not the heathen in Africa or Asia or the Eskimos in Alaska. Not the people we disagree with or who do things differently than we do. All need to see a living demonstration of what God can do in the heart of an individual, a marriage, and a family. We have a responsibility to gain the experience Christ offers and then to share it to the extent that God opens the way. Let there be no disguise to the pain we see in our communities. Society is a mess. The world is hurting. *Lord, open my heart to see and not ignore the cries of the world in need. Lord, help me to help one person today.*

How must Christ feel when He looks upon our world and sees those who have been blessed with abundant spiritual resources—yet who are reluctant to yield themselves to become practical demonstrations of God's irresistible grace to those who are languishing in spiritual darkness?

If you have read this book, then God is calling you to apply the principles and gain the experiences discussed in these pages so that you are equipped to share this vision with others. We have a moral obligation to experience irresistible marriages—and then to proclaim what we're experiencing. God doesn't *ask* us to go—He *commands* us to go! " 'And this gospel of the kingdom will be preached in all the world.' "[2] Which gospel? *"This gospel."* The gospel that is changing you. The gospel that is making your marriage irresistible and reconnecting your family. So when you start to experience God filling your life, share that experience with someone else. If a need comes to your attention and you have the resources to help and there is no check in your conscience from God, then help!

Your circle of influence

Every one of us has a pulpit, whether or not we are preachers. Our influence is our pulpit. And this pulpit goes with us everywhere we go—our homes, the grocery store, the airport, work, and church. What are you preaching in your pulpit? Does your life and marriage match your profession? Don't misunderstand. I'm *not* saying that we must be perfect in all things in order to share with others. But we must be faithful to follow God. Are you passing on what is helping you, encouraging you, lifting you up?

After Stan and Susan experienced their marriage becoming irresistible, they couldn't stop talking about it! Family, friends, church members, and fellow employees all heard the word of their "testimony." As a result, five couples showed up at one of our Empowered Living camp meetings that

---

2. Matthew 24:14.

very year. We had the privilege of counseling with two of them and chatting with the other three. Guess what? Stan's and Susan's testimony helped their friends find the same freedom they had found—the freedom to love and to be loved unconditionally! You see, the gospel—the good news—goes beyond a well-defined system of truth. That's good and needs to be there. But the good news goes beyond doctrine and theology to finding a power in Christ that is able to liberate you to love extravagantly.

At the camp meeting, I asked Stan and Susan to briefly share their testimony. Hundreds of people were affected. Women, tears of hope mingled with their doubts, and men with awakened consciences were encouraged to apply the principles of an irresistible marriage to their lives. I don't know the final outcome of Stan's and Susan's testimony, but I know that marriages are going to be in the kingdom that got their start from the willingness of this couple to share—vulnerably share. They shared honestly who they were, what their marriage had been, what they discovered, and how they implemented the changes that infused their marriage with a better way of life.

Is God asking you to do the same? Don't say it's too early in your experience to share.

The demoniacs whom Jesus delivered began sharing what little they understood about His power on the very day they found their freedom. In fact, because of the testimony of these two men, a whole town came out to see and hear the One who had transformed their lives. Now, if they had started preaching the gospel while demons still controlled them, they wouldn't have been too credible. But as soon as they experienced the change that Jesus worked in their hearts, they began to share.

You can do that too. Apply His principles, taste His grace—and then share so that others who are too afraid or embarrassed to ask will receive the word of your testimony and have the opportunity to experiment whether these things will work for them.

God will prompt you. Your conscience will prick you to say a word in season. Don't be embarrassed. Where would you be today if someone else had not *passed it on*? What if that person had been unwilling to be vulnerable with you? Scripture says that Andrew told Peter.[3] Philip told Nathanael.[4] What if they had not *passed it on*? This is God's ordained method of reaching untold numbers. Start a chain reaction with the couples you know. Rise above the social gospel and dare to go deep. Dare to be vulnerable.

---

3. John 1:40, 41.
4. Verse 45.

Bill and Barbara were so enthusiastic that they bought a case of *Empowered Living* books, passed them out, and started a small marriage-renewal group on Wednesday nights. They assigned a chapter for the individuals in the group to read on their own, and then they met to discuss the questions and exercises at the end of the chapter. Week after week, this group met to share and encourage one another. Sometimes they spent two or three weeks on one chapter. These people were so loaded with real-life circumstances that no one wanted to move on until they had covered all the points. A lot of honest disclosure took place—often accompanied by tears. So often, we feel that we are the only ones who are struggling. When we find out we are not alone, we can draw strength from each other. A small group can provide someone to talk with, share with—someone who understands and becomes an encourager on life's journey.

Rady and Jeanette sent out a letter to everyone on their Christmas list, announcing the good news of their marriage renewal. They shared their testimony at camp meeting and at our open house—and other couples were encouraged to see that they were not alone and that God could change them too. Rady and Jeanette also started a small group to help couples address the issues in their marriages and to encourage them that God's principles work when they are applied.

Another couple I know invites one couple at a time to their home and shares with them one DVD from the Empowered Living seminar. If the couple is interested in what is presented, they continue the series. If not, they share with someone else.

Perhaps you can present a vespers program at church and give your testimony. Perhaps you can hand out books or booklets, play DVDs, or share CDs. Don't wait until you feel your marriage is on track to start a small group. Studying and sharing with others, receiving their encouragement, prayers, and feedback can help you and your spouse work through your own difficult areas while you are helping and encouraging others.

The gospel is not merely to be spread by the preachers, evangelists, and missionaries. You have a part no one else can play. You can be a witness to people no one else can reach. Everyone has a responsibility, not only to God, but to their brothers and sisters, to share their testimony with others.

I don't know what God is asking you to do. That's between you and Him. I do know He doesn't want you to be like the Dead Sea—only taking in and never letting out. Neither does He want you to be like a drained reservoir—giving until you're all dried up, while not receiving what you need yourself. God wants us to be like Bowman Lake—a lake in Glacier National Park just across the river from our home. Bowman Lake is surrounded by snow-capped peaks and ancient glaciers that fill it constantly with the crystal clear streams that tumble down the mountainsides through evergreen forests. The lake is fresh and full of life. Beavers build their lodges, otters frolic in the sunshine, fish flourish. I've watched bear saunter along the edges, deer come down for a drink, and eagles dive for fish. It's a place of beauty that just draws you to it! Out of this abundance flows a crystal clear stream to nourish the valley below.

That's what a true Christian's life is meant to be—constantly receiving life from God through the various resources He provides and then passing these blessings on! I've come to see that as I give to others, God gives me more in return. He multiplies the talents that I use. What a joy it is to be a tool in God's hands and to see others' lives affected just as mine has been!

Back to the present

"I now pronounce you man and wife! What God has joined together let not man put asunder." My thoughts were jolted back to J. D. and Alecia. They stood facing each other while the minister stared at them for what seemed like a long time. Finally, J. D. whispered something to his grandpa—the minister. Grandpa looked a bit mystified, so Alecia leaned over and repeated it. Grandpa still didn't catch on, so J. D. and Alecia shrugged their shoulders, threw their arms around each other, and enjoyed their first married kiss. The audience erupted with clapping and cheers.

The new couple started down the steps toward the back of the church, when all of a sudden, J. D. stopped, turned to his glowing bride, and then swooped her up in his arms and carried her down the aisle while everyone cheered again! (I asked him later if he had planned that and he said No.)

Irresistible—that's J. D. and Alecia! Irresistible again—that's Sally and me, Stan and Susan, Bill and Barbara, Rady and Jeanette. It can be you too! And when it is, pass it on!

Study Questions for Chapter 10

1. Is God asking you to share your testimony?
2. What does the phrase " 'they did not love their lives to the death' " mean to you? (Revelation 12:11).
3. Is God impressing you to share the principles that are changing your marriage?
4. Is God moving upon you to start a small group study? Hand out some books? Show some DVDs or share a CD? Reach out to a different culture?

BONUS CHAPTER

Guidelines for Young Lovers

*Ponder the path of your feet,
And let all your ways be established.*

—Proverbs 4:26

Young people often approach Sally and me with variations of the same basic question: "How can I know if a person I like will be a good spouse for me?" Or parents of young people ask us, "What are some guidelines to help our son or daughter make a wise choice for a future mate?"

It's hard to overestimate the importance of this question. Whom a person decides to marry is one of the most critical decisions of life. You can trade cars, sell your house, or change occupations without too much turmoil. But changing your spouse shreds the fabric of something God Himself has joined together into a seamless unity—namely, your two hearts and lives—and has huge ramifications both for this life and for eternity.

This was an important issue to Sally and me as our boys developed relationships with girls during their teen years. All four of us talked about it at length during our evening family times, and we encouraged our boys to write down a list of qualities they felt were important in a future spouse. In our counseling, we encourage young people to do this, too—and to do it before they become emotionally involved with someone. Otherwise, the "love cocktail" we talked about in chapter 1 can really skew their ideas of what they are looking for![1]

After a number of years, we have identified seven factors young people should consider in putting together such a list:

- shared values
- compatibility

---

1. Sample lists that others have shared with us appear at the end of this chapter.

- adaptability
- spirituality
- "spark"
- a thirty-day "discovery program"
- God's leading

Shared values

There are four main areas to explore in terms of shared values: religion, lifestyle, parenting, and life goals. It's not necessary that you and your future mate have identical values in every category, but you must determine what areas you each consider to be negotiable—and nonnegotiable. This can help to prevent some difficult adjustments later in life.

Religion: It's a good idea to find someone with whom you share the same religious convictions. When two people marry who have differing religions, they often experience horrendous problems after marriage. They find themselves in conflict over raising the children, their social life, and their outlook on life. Don't fall for the illusion that you can marry this person and then convert him or her to your way of thinking. It rarely happens.

Lifestyle: If one of you loves a quiet country life with a simple, pleasant, and practical home, while the other craves the excitement of the city and a showy mansion, it will be next to impossible to find a situation that accommodates both preferences. If one of you is a saver, while the other is a spender, can you work together to balance each other—or will you always be at odds? Do you agree on the issue of debt?

What about gender-role expectations? Does one of you have rigid ideas about what is man's work and what is woman's work or will you work out a way to mutually help each other?

Maybe one of you likes lots of social activities and frequent interaction with friends and family, while the other prefers solitude and quiet. What about entertainment and relaxation? Do you have similar tastes and values about TV and videos? Would you rather go for a walk and talk—or read a book together?

Does one of you place a high value on staying physically fit, while the other prefers to be a couch potato? Do you share the same dietary convictions? Do you both like to eat out or would you rather eat at home?

What are your tastes in recreation? Does one love the out-of-doors, while the other would rather go to the opera? Where do you each stand when it comes to competitive sports? Would you rather watch from the sidelines, get involved, or avoid competition altogether? What do you expect from a spouse?

How do you like to vacation? Does one of you like to travel to exotic places, tour museums and art galleries, and stay in ritzy hotels, while the other prefers to throw a pack on his back and head for the mountains? Can you enjoy accommodating each other's preferences?

What are your standards for dress style? What is important to you to see in your potential mate?

Parenting: What qualities are important to you in a prospective father or mother of your children? Do you need your future mate to be a strong disciplinarian or to be more nurturing? What parenting style was he or she raised with—and how will that affect his or her approach to child rearing? Will that approach be compatible with your parenting style and expectations?

Do the two of you agree about how you will educate your children—public school versus church school versus homeschooling? Do you expect to send your children to college?

Goals: What are your dreams and goals in life? If your ambition is to become a career missionary to the Tibetan plateau, and your spouse wants to build a Fortune 500 company, you will find yourselves at odds no matter how great the tingles feel initially.

Compatibility

When considering a future mate, you should look for someone who is 85 percent compatible with you in most areas of life. For example, if you are 100 percent compatible in your ideas about recreation, but find only 25 percent compatibility in the other major areas of everyday life, it won't be enough to make for happy daily living.

With this in mind, candidly evaluate the following differences or similarities:

- Introverted versus extroverted.
- Scheduled and timely versus late and spur of the moment.
- Neat and tidy versus scattered and messy.
- A communicator versus a noncommunicator.
- Lighthearted versus overly rigid.
- Tolerant versus intolerant.

In addition, you should look at such areas as finances and spending habits, spiritual drive and experience, decision-making techniques, attitudes toward socializing, community and church involvement, shopping and spending habits, and how you display physical affection. It's also important that you consider compatibility in your weaknesses as well as your strengths.

Adaptability

When two people marry, each brings to the marriage his or her own expectations of married life—both conscious and subconscious. There will be differences arising from the way each has been raised. It's important to recognize that in the new marriage, life can't be all your way—and it can't be all your future spouse's way. You will need to blend your two ways into a new marriage that reflects who the two of you are and who you will become.

Are you and your potential mate reasonably adaptable? If not, you will have a much harder road to live and walk. Each of you needs to have a reasonable willingness to give and take, to grow and mature in your lifestyle.

A lot of your success in this area will be determined by how both of you solve problems. Do you each have the skill to lovingly confront the areas needing to be addressed—or do you tend to avoid them? Is one of you a "talker" while the other is the "strong, silent type"? Can you both admit to being wrong when you've been in the wrong? Does one of you tend to be logical while keeping emotions tucked away—or too emotional without the balance of logic?

Adaptability is a willingness to work through difficulties for the mutual good of the relationship without insisting that it has to be all one's own way. Both partners in a marriage need to adapt themselves to the other for the common good of the relationship.

Spirituality

Belonging to the same religious persuasion and being on the same page spiritually can be two different things—and both are important to evaluate prior to marriage. Someone can cling tenaciously to a correct system of doctrine, be very conscientious in religious duties, and zealously advocate spiritual truth. But, in and of themselves, these things will not lay the foundation for marital harmony—even if you agree on 85 percent of them.

Remember principle one that we talked about in chapter 2? Both you and your potential spouse need a daily, living, personal walk with God. You should be able to see tangible evidence that self is dying daily and becoming God-governed rather than man-managed and self-directed.

Does your potential mate seek God daily—both alone and with you—to help you to learn how to handle conflict, disagreements, and all the stumbling stones you come upon in life's roadway?

"Spark"

After evaluating all of the above, ask yourself: Do we have a "spark" between us? Is there a heart-to-heart attraction between us? Are we drawn toward each other physically, emotionally, and spiritually?

Do I enjoy his personality? Do I like her sense of humor and the sound of her laugh? Is he into mischief all the time? Is he serious or is he a nice balance of the two? Is she always focused or is she free-spirited? Is he a leader or a servant? Is she amiable or analytical? Is he or she a blend of the above qualities, and do I like that? How does he or she match my personality?

Is there a two-way attraction between you? Is the "spark" mutual? If you are a woman, make sure the man you are considering loves you for who you are and not for your physical attributes only. If you are a man, be sure that your girlfriend isn't just looking for security. Make sure she loves you for you!

Writing your list of desirable qualities in a future spouse may take time—and it will probably change as you grow and learn more about yourself and relationships. Be open with God and individuals you trust about what is realistic and nonnegotiable in your expectations.

Discovery—a thirty-day program

Dating has its downsides. You both dress up, apply perfume or cologne, put your best foot forward, and go out to eat—and you think, *This is great! This is what I'm looking for!*

But what comes out when your best foot is forward may not be the real you. You can disguise the real you on a date or over a weekend. You might not do this intentionally—but it takes a real-life scenario to really get to know each other. I suggest that once you've covered these first five areas and feel you are really interested in pursuing the relationship further, you need to schedule a thirty-day discovery program.

Invite the other person to come and live in your parents' home with you for thirty days—then go live with him or her in their parents' home for thirty days. Here you will encounter real life. You get up and go to bed together—separate rooms, of course! You eat together, do dishes together, go to work together, play together, clean house together, and share all the daily responsibilities of life together.

You get to see how the other person's family operates and how he or she relates to parents, brothers, sisters, workmates, and employers. You get to see more of who the real person is—or isn't.

This discovery program isn't about picking apart the other person; it's about really getting to know them. When you discover some imbalances, you have the opportunity to work them through or realize that there is a basic incompatibility. It's a wonderful blessing to get this information before the wedding! Too many people wait to get it *after* the wedding.

Pray that God reveals to you all you need to see and know in these thirty days of deep discovery.

If you're living away from home, have a full-time job, and find it's not practical to take your friend home for thirty days, find a creative alternative so that you have the opportunity to find out as much as you can about who this person is behind closed doors. For instance, you might arrange to spend a few days or a week at the home of some mature friends. In one case I'm familiar with, the young lady was working at her grandma's place. The young man who was interested in her stayed with a friend down the street. He would come over every day and help her with her chores. They developed a genuine friendship, but also discovered in the process that they were not well suited for each other as marriage partners.

God's leading

God's leading should be both the foundation and the capstone of your decision to get married. Your own desires and emotions or the matchmaking of other well-intentioned people are not safe guides. Only God knows if the two of you are right for each other.

Advice from parents, family, and friends is helpful—but it must be screened through God to know whether it is from Him. The final decision rests between you and God.

God is willing to guide us in all the affairs of life—especially in this one decision upon which so much depends! If you decide to honor God supremely and refuse to step forward without His blessing, He will make His will known to you through providential leading, input from others, guidance from His Word, and His impressions on your conscience. Pray, pray, pray! If you are in the habit of praying twice a day, pray *four* times a day when you are contemplating marriage.

And take your time! The old saying is true: "Marry in haste; repent at leisure." Take time to know yourself. Take time to know your prospective mate. Take time to know God's will and understand His leading.

Love God supremely with your whole heart, soul, strength, and mind. Learn to walk with Him in a practical way by developing your talents, personality, skills, and abilities.

Cultivate relationships that have spiritual and emotional depth with people who are not potential marriage partners—people of varying ages (from eighteen to eighty) and of both genders. These might be grandparents, aunts or uncles, an employer, a neighbor, or a friend. This has two benefits: First, it will help you develop wholesome relationship skills in real-life settings and to become as whole and healthy as you can be. Then you will tend to attract partners who are also whole and healthy—or at least you will be able to recognize those who are not compatible and with whom you will not be able to build an irresistible marriage.

Second, building such relationships can help you discover more about what kind of personalities you are, or aren't, compatible with. What is it about Grandma you've always liked? What is it about your uncle that feels like a fingernail scratching on a chalkboard? What you learn in real relationships will help you to refine your list of what is essential for you to find in the one you eventually marry.

Two books that can help you in this process are *Before You Get Engaged* by David and Brent Gudgel and *Boundaries in Dating* by Henry Cloud and John Townsend.

God bless you as you seek to find His will and an irresistible marriage! Now for those lists:

Essential Qualities ("Must Have's") in a Wife[2]

List 1:
1. Must be a firm, Bible-believing Christian who belongs to my denomination.
2. Must have a close experiential walk with the Lord.
3. Must believe and have confidence in the Spirit of Prophecy.
4. Must have a winsome personality.
5. Must not be afraid to speak up when needed.
6. Must believe in proper child discipline.
7. Must dress modestly, but in a tasteful way.
8. Must love nature and like to do things outdoors.
9. Must be athletic to a certain degree—not weak or frail.
10. Must be very attractive to me.
11. Must be in shape—not overweight.
12. Must be a vegetarian.
13. Must like kids, family, and people in general, and like to help others.
14. Must be willing to go wherever or do whatever the Lord directs us to do.
15. Must be able to stretch a dollar.
16. Must be able to live without modern conveniences if required, i.e., if we were to live in a foreign country as missionaries for a certain length of time.

---

2. Remember, these lists are examples of some we have seen in our counseling over the years. Your list of essential qualities will vary with your personality and outlook on life. The lists given here are designed to help you begin thinking about what you feel are essential qualities in a mate. Remember, too, when listing your essential qualities in a spouse—no one is *perfect*!

17. Must be able to give good back and foot rubs.
18. Must have some knowledge of natural remedies—or be willing to learn.
19. Must be a neat housekeeper.
20. Must not get easily moody or depressed.
21. Must love living in the country.
22. Must have some type of working skills in case she would have to earn an income.
23. Must have a conservative taste in music.
24. Must show good temperance in appetite, speech, etc.
25. Must not be older than me.
26. Must not be more than three years younger than me.
27. Must like my parents and get along well with them.
28. Must be someone who can motivate me when I need it.
29. Must like to cook wholesome food.
30. Must be thoughtful of others.
31. Must not be a homebody type—not the type that wants to stay home all the time.
32. Must be able to sing.
33. Must show wisdom and give good counsel.
34. Must be someone who can listen.
35. If and when—must want to homeschool our children.
36. Must be someone who remains calm under stress and doesn't panic.

List 2:
1. Reserved.
2. Loyal.
3. Follows good leadership.
4. Even-keeled.
5. Sweet.
6. Tidy.
7. Timely.
8. Playful.
9. Physically active.
10. Adventuresome.
11. Gentle.
12. Hard worker.
13. Able to learn.
14. Is there for me.
15. Possesses a "freshness."

16. Pure.
17. Able to run a household.
18. Likes to live decently.
19. Spiritual.
20. Able to "go deep."
21. Attractive.
22. At least two inches, but not more than four inches, shorter than me.
23. Slim build.
24. Hair not too long and not too short.
25. Discerning.
26. Fairly decisive.
27. Fair.
28. Won't follow bad leadership.
29. Can challenge without being overbearing.
30. Efficient.
31. No unreasonable fears.
32. Enjoys outdoor adventure and recreation.
33. Enjoys the quiet.
34. Flexible.
35. Able to take a "No."

List 3:
1. Must have a good Christian experience:
   - Be striving upward—although not perfect.
   - Live like a Christian in daily life—dress, word, and deed.
   - Be serious about her Christian experience.
   - Make spirituality a priority of life.
2. Must love and enjoy children—not just babies:
   - Deal with them in a Christian manner when they disobey or get on her nerves.
   - Play with them and enjoy it.
   - Teach and train them versus "Do what I say."
3. Must be able to skillfully carry her share of life's duties:
   - Keep the home clean.
   - Keep the home running smoothly.
   - Make tasty, good-looking, healthful food.
   - Be timely in carrying out her duties.
   - Be efficient—like Grandma.
4. Must not be generally moody:
   - Have a good positive attitude whether feeling good or not.

- Not completely feelings-oriented.
- Have enough emotion to keep love active and special.
5. Must not be overly conservative in dress and food.
6. Must be enjoyable to be around:
    - Not too quiet; not too outspoken.
    - Not loud or boisterous or a "take-charge" personality.
    - Ready to be quiet and be a shadow when necessary.
    - Speak up and make meaningful conversation—not just chitchat.
7. Must be able to laugh and enjoy my company—and show it in little ways.
8. Must love the out-of-doors—but not at the expense or neglect of home duties.
9. Must be willing to be challenged and try new things.
10. Must have a "serving" personality:
    - Watch over me without being in charge.
    - Be sensitive to my needs.
    - Foresee those needs and happily fill them.
11. Have an "objective" personality:
    - Think things through logically.
    - Respond to emergency situations instead of reacting.
12. Must be supportive—even when she disagrees:
    - Willing to talk over hard issues instead of avoiding them.
    - Discuss issues versus adopting the "silent treatment."
    - Willing to come to a unified agreement.
13. Must be economical with finances:
    - Not too stingy.
    - Build up savings in good times.
    - Not caught up in "shopping."
    - Buy good quality.
14. Must be active and lively:
    - Not always wanting to sleep.
    - Be somewhat mischievous, but not overdo it.
15. Must work willingly with her hands:
    - Sew and mend clothing as needed.
    - Decorate the interior of the home.
    - Landscape around the home with a woman's touch.
16. Must be "beautiful":
    - Inwardly, more importantly than outwardly.
    - In character.
    - In personality.
    - Physically attractive.

17. Must be compatible in life goals, lifestyle, values, and principles.
18. Must be a great:
    - Mother.
    - Wife.
    - Homeschool teacher.
    - Housekeeper.
    - Lover.
19. Must be loved by my parents and family.
20. Must be planning on a life-long, happy union:
    - Here, as well as in heaven.
    - Take love to a newer and higher level.
    - Continue special attentions after the courtship is over.
21. Must be younger than me.
22. Must have a willingness to do whatever it takes to make the family successful.
23. Must be willing to share home duties.
24. Must be willing to go wherever God may call.

Essential Qualities ("Must Have's") in a Husband

List 1:
1. God-directed, spiritual, principled in life and habits.
2. Have a heart for God's people—sharing with others what he has experienced in his own walk with God.
3. Have a "leader" personality—a stronger personality than mine.
4. Tested and trustworthy—honest.
5. Adaptable under God.
6. A wise financial manager and provider; have a solid occupation.
7. Neat, orderly, and organized.
8. Clean cut, well-dressed.
9. Fit, athletic, active, and adventurous.
10. Temperate in lifestyle and diet.
11. A man who wins my heart by first becoming my best friend.
12. Someone I can respect and admire.
13. Fun-loving, playful, and romantic.
14. Someone I love to be with and have a great attraction to.
15. Well built, muscular.
16. A wise gentleness that balances his firmness to work with my personality and needs.

Guidelines for Young Lovers

17. Good with children.
18. Loves canoeing and camping.
19. Musically talented.
20. Older than I am.

List 2:
1. A man of God—spiritual. Question: Is he a man who has—and is—giving God the leadership of his life?
   - Learning of Him.
   - Led by Him.
   - Leading others to Him.
2. A "leader" personality. Question: Is he a man who has the bearing of a leader, someone who will provide for his family's needs, lead his family spiritually, take the lead in home matters—teaching us by example, training, and precept to stand alone in God?
   - Has a leadership presence and bearing.
   - Is a "go-getter," a man of action.
   - A provider.
   - Stands alone with God.
3. Healthy and active in lifestyle—a picture of manhood. Question: Does he have the commitment and drive to let God direct his appetite and habits? Does he take a natural delight in outdoor activities?
   - Physically fit.
   - A sportsman.
   - Adventurous.
   - Self-controlled.
4. Compatible, suitable—a man for me. Question: Has God kindled in my heart a flame of attraction, mingled with a sparkling compatibility, that draws me to him—and he to me?
   - Attraction—"spark."
   - Blendable personalities.
   - Adaptable.
   - Depth.

List 3:
Spiritual concerns:
   - Loves Christ above all else.
   - His highest goal is to follow God's leading.
   - His fruits show a spiritual connection with God.

- Consults God when problems arise.
- Has a deep, spiritual devotional life.
- Listens for God's voice.

As priest of our family:
- Family is a high priority.
- Leads out in family worship and memorizing Scripture.
- Is kind and affectionate to children.
- Will discipline his family under God.
- Plays with children.
- Is tender and loving.
- Makes wise financial decisions.
- Is financially secure.

In relationship to his wife:
- Shows me respect.
- Lifts me closer to God.
- Tells me kindly when I'm in the wrong.
- Comforts, supports, and guides me.
- Shows me his love throughout the day.

In relationship to his parents:
- Loves his parents.
- Honors and respects them.
- Listens to their guidance.

Personal qualities:
- Honest—personally and in business.
- Communicates well.
- Listens to what others have to say.
- Has high goals—but is realistic.
- Is able to achieve the goals he sets.
- Willingly accepts failure and tries again.
- Doesn't get discouraged easily.
- Loves the outdoors and outdoor activities.
- Encourages his family to take part in outdoor activities.
- Is physically fit.

Want to Know MORE About the Hohnbergers?

Empowered Living Ministries is the outgrowth of Jim and Sally's experience with God. Located near Glacier National Park, the ministry office is here to serve your needs, whether it is to book a speaking engagement, request a media appearance, or order any of a large variety of resource materials, including books, booklets, and seminars on CD or DVD. For more information, contact:

Empowered Living Ministries
3945 North Fork Road
Columbia Falls, MT 59912

EMPOWEREDLIVINGMINISTRIES.ORG

Phone 406-387-4333
Orders 877-755-8300
Fax 406-387-4336